Eno Glas

The Shaman and me

An unique story full of insight,
magic and adventure

Bibliographic information of the German National Library

Deutsche Bibliothek lists this publication in the German National Bibliography; detailed bibliographic data is available on the Internet at dnb.dnb.de.

TWENTYSIX-The self-publishing publisher

A cooperation between Verlagsgruppe RandomHouse and BoD-Books on Demand

©2020 Eno Glas

Production and publishing:
BoD - Books on Demand, Norderstedt
ISBN: 9783740715823

Before leaving India, Michael Jackson penned down this beautiful note on a pillow...

India, all my live I have longed to see your face.

I met you and your people and fell in love with you.

Now my heart is filled with sorrow and despair for I have to leave, but I promise I shall return to love you and caress you again.

Your kindness has overwhelmed me, your spiritual awareness has moved me, and your children have truly touched my heart. They are the face of God.

I truly love and adore you India. Forever, continue to love, heal and educate the children, the future shines on them.

You are my special love, India.

Forever, may God always bless you.

Michael Jackson

On my extensive travels and during my stays in India I once met a European Swami who lived in this country for almost thirty years.

This meeting became the most intense, instructive and adventurous time in my life so far.

This story is about that time.

Open your eyes, read and follow the images of your own film...

It was a coincidence or maybe it wasn't. I was on a walk along a lonely, sandy beach in South India, enjoying the first nice weather after the dull, grey monsoon. The golden yellow sand glittered in the sun. The whitecaps of the waves seemed snow white.

The destination of my walk was an ancient cashew nut tree which grew near the beach. Under this tree I experienced some years ago a wonderful day and an unforgettable night of love together with Caroline, an Australian traveler.

Cashew nut trees are often grown in a way, so that the branches reach to the ground, creating a natural hollow space, similar to a tent or a dome.

This one I wanted to visit had grown especially beautiful and lush into a big green half dome. Inside, not visible from the outside, was an almost circular room, several steps wide and about ten feet high. In the middle stud a triple trunk.

I wonder if the tree was still standing after all these years. Maybe the farmers had cut it down and burned it...but no, there it was. I saw it already from a distance, beautiful as ever in all his grace and splendor. For a moment I stood in front of it, thinking and remembered of those wonderful times back then - I wonder what happened to Caroline? Whether she has children, is married, leads a normal, settled life? As I was now wallowing in old memories, I slowly parted the branches out of the way and entered the inside of the tree...I was almost struck by a blow: In the middle of the room sat a rather wild looking old guy, naked, dressed with only one string thong, on a raffia mat in a cross-legged yoga position. The guy might be in his se-venties or eighties. He wore a white, bushy Santa Claus beard that reached down to his chest. The wrinkled face was framed by grey felted hair, from which yello-wish, sun-bleached dreadlocks grew. The body of the old man seemed to consist only of wrinkles, bones, tendons and muscles which were covered by a brown, leathery skin.

"Hello...am...am, I am sorry," I stammered, "I don't want to disturb...Actually, I wasn't expecting anyone here."

"No problem," replied the old man, "I don't feel disturbed, it rather seems to me that maybe my presence here is disturbing you?"

"No, no...I'm just a little frightened, you don't meet a naked man from the west under a tree here in India in such a remote area every day!"

"Likewise, here in India in such a remote area a white man does not walk often into a tree just like that every day", the old man bawled from an almost toothless mouth. "Come sit down, would you like a glass of lemon water?" he asked.

"Oh yes, I'd love to, it's very hot walking along the beach, the sun is already very high."

I took a seat on the raffia mat. With a half coconut shell the old man scooped a glass of water out of a big clay jug, into which he pressed half a lime and stirred in a pinch of salt.

"By the way, I am Swami Sathyanandapuri, they also call me Shaman Swami. But just call me Swami", he introduced himself.

"My name is Eno."

"Pleased to meet you! From which country do you come from, Eno, and what brings you to India under this tree?"

"I come from Switzerland. I know this tree from the past, under it I experienced a wonderful night of love together with an Australian traveler some years ago. I thought, since I'm in the area, I'd stop by to visit our love tree again."

"And then, instead of a super woman with great curves", the Swami grumbled, clapping his hand on his thigh, "you run in to naked, toothless, wrinkled old grandpa! No wonder you're so scared."

We both had to laugh.

"Tell me, where are you from, Swami", I continued, "and what are you doing here in India under this tree, is this your meditation place?" "I was born in Germany eighty-two years ago. Since thirty years I live as a beggar monk in India. This tree is my home, under it I have lived and slept for almost a year. I even survived the monsoon here. I simply stretched a plastic tarpaulin over the three big branches there and didn't get a single drop off."

"Wow...thirty years in India", I marveled, "a long time! And from what do you live on, how do you make a living?"

"As I said, I earn my living as a mendicant. At the great Shiva Temple in Tiruvannamalai. A huge festival takes place every full moon, often attended by thousands of believers and pilgrims from all over India. There I beg so much money in each case that it comfortably is enough until the next full moon. The pilgrims are very generous, they make such a pilgrimage only once in their life."

"Hm...a strange vocation for a man from the west, to live in India as a beggar," I answered musing.

"I am not just an ordinary beggar", the Swami explained, "I have the status of a Swami, Guru, Shaman and Yogi here in India. I live voluntarily as a beggar monk, it's my job, my vocation, you understand? What kind of work do you do, Eno?" he asked me.

"Well...I have tried and started a lot of things, nothing could satisfy in the long run, everything became boring, routine and grey everyday life. My last job was as a stage technician in a big city theatre. For a while I was the singer of a pop band and an artist. The band broke up, nobody wanted my paintings...In short, Swami, I am searching for the meaning, the vocation and the love of my life."

"All right", said the Swami nodded his head. "At least you know what you're looking for! Are you travelling alone here in India or is there a woman waiting for you in some hotel room or beach bungalow?" he wanted to know.

"No, I'm travelling solo, there's a woman in Switzerland - Erica is her name. We have been together for two years more or less... Love is a complicated story. How about you Swami, with love, have you found it?"

"I can't complain," he said with a smile, "You must have thought that such an old Yogi lives in celibacy. I'm together with Lisa, an American woman, for the last seven years now. Lisa left for Kolkata two weeks ago, she is attending a Yoga school there for the next three, four, months."

In my mind I imagined an old, toothless, funny female similar to the Swami, with felted grey dreadlocks, at an age Yoga class.

"Would you like to see a picture of her?" he asked me and handed me a photo which he kept in a book between the pages.

"Wow...Swami, where did you pick this lady up?"

"Amazed, aren't you, Eno? You probably thought I was dating an old, nagging witch."

"Well, not exactly, but I didn't think you were dating a thirty-year old supermodel, Swami."

"Lisa is thirty-three years old, we met seven years ago at the great Shiva temple in Tiruvannamalai. I had actually finished with the women - but in life things often turn out differently than one thinks."

"Does she also live here under the tree?" I asked.

"You want to know everything exactly, hey," shouted the Swami. "No, she has another room in town. She lives here and there. Lisa is a great lady", he enthused.

"Crazy guy", I thought - lives in India as a beggar monk, counts eighty-two winters and has such a girlfriend!?

Because I had an appointment with my friend Angelo in town for lunch, I soon had to leave and say goodbye to the Swami. When I wanted to donate him a 100 Rupee note, he refused with thanks.

"You were my guest, Eno. I don't accept money from my guests. It was nice meeting you. Come by again. You are always welcome at my place and at your tree."

I thanked him for his hospitality and promised to drop by again.

Because I was a bit late, I took a small footpath up to the road, which was half a mile away. With a motor rickshaw I was chauffeured directly to Pondicherry to the restaurant Ashok, where Angelo was already sitting at the table and waiting for me. - Angelo is an old friend from my home town. Together we started this trip to India two months ago. Because Angelo wanted to stay a little longer in Puri, we separated for a while and met again in Pondicherry.

We ordered a fish curry with rice side dish, chapatis and a cool Kingfisher-beer. At dinner I told him about my meeting with the Shaman-Swami.

"You are a lucky man", he said enthusiastically, "you don't run into a Swami-Shaman like that every day. It is certainly no coincidence that you just met him under your old love tree - that is a special sign, certainly not a coincidence, it almost looks as if you had been ordered and he was waiting for you."

"You think so? Sounds a bit far-fetched...but who knows...this Swami reminds me most of an old hippie from the sixties who somehow got stuck in India. - Amazing that the old man is together with such a young woman...but Osho was also together with Shila..."

"You see, Eno, the guy is a magician, tantric, guru, Shaman and Swami, the guy is certainly wise and enlightened", Angelo said enthusiastically.

"Well..." I replied skeptical, "obviously, the old man has gone through a lot in his long life, he is certainly a wise old man in his own way - but he is hardly not omniscient and enlightened."

"But perhaps Eno, he is close to it. You should definitely visit this Swami again."

"I'll certainly do that...on that occasion I'll find out how close he is."

Angelo and I stayed the whole afternoon in the same cozy rooftop garden restaurant under sun umbrellas with coffee, lassis and cake. We discussed about love, life, vocation, about God and the world. We came to the conclusion that true love and true vocation are probably the most desirable things in life. But we also realized that only few people actually achieved these goals.

"Eno, as you know, I've been attending a Yoga school for a week now, there are still places available, don't you want to join? The Yoga teacher is a great guy, he's got it down pat, his name is Vijai, one of the best!"

"Hmm...I don't know. Yoga would definitely suit me, but somehow, I lack the motivation to do it or maybe I'm just too lazy. How about the women? You got any hot chicks in your yoga class?" I wanted to know.

"You're still the same, Eno - always after the chicks! Sure, there are some great women, they are so agile, against them you are a stiff stick!"

"That's just what they need - a stiff stick", I joked and laughed."

"Spare me your chauvinistic and macho behavior", Angelo waved off with a grin and gave me a light boxer on the upper arm "I'm off," he said, "the yoga class starts in an hour, I have to take a shower."

We said goodbye. I went to my room in the Amala-Lodge, washed some laundry there and rested a little while. I had dinner at the Indian Coffeehouse where I ate a huge *Masala-Dosa*. For dessert I relaxingly enjoyed a coffee and leaned back. The fans were spinning in their circles. The flies flew humming their curves and the waiters shuffled around the tables with silver trays. In front of the open entrance portal stood a few ragged beggars. A halting chaos of cars, rickshaws, pedestrians, bicycles and holy cows moved along the dusty road.

Some days later, while shopping at the fruit market, I spontaneously had the idea to visit the Swami and bring him some fruits. The fruit market was very crowded, it was hectic and loud. I was the only Westerner who stood out accordingly. The market women screamed, laughed, waved and cackled for my favor. I was bargain at about five sales stands at the same time, got pretty stressed and annoyed at the end. The market women had their bright joy. As consolation, one of the women gave me three limes, another one put a small flower garland around my neck. I was touched, the stress was forgotten. At the next cycle shop I rented a bicycle and rode the five miles along the road, down the narrow footpath directly to Swami's tree.

"Good afternoon, Swami, hello", I greeted him, "I hope I'm not disturbing you. I thought I'd stop by and bring you some fruits."

"Gee...Eno, you're just in time, welcome. I was just going up to the village to buy bananas and limes. Come on, let's make a fruit salad."

The Swami fetched an aluminum pot, knife, spoon and two plates, then he carefully began to peel the pineapple, papaya, apples and bananas. I cut them into slices, wheels and dices. At the end we drizzled lime juice over it, mixed some sugar and grated coconut in to. The fruit salad tasted delicious. "Like Ambrosia" the Swami said.

I told him about my discussion with Angelo in which we had found out that without a true vocation, without a true love, you could never be truly happy, that it would be the most important thing in life is to strive and seek for it.

"Well done, for two youngsters not so bad", nodded the Swami appreciatively, "you've found out quite a lot. After all, that is already two thirds of the essence. To true love and true vocation comes the true truth - all good things come in threes!"

"Where and how do I find the real truth, Swami? There are so many truths, ideologies, religions and world views, how can anyone keep track of them? - Everyone thinks he owns the truth!"

"Ask that a detective who is currently working on a tricky criminal case, he as well is looking for the truth in his case, he too, like me, has to secure traces, uncover lies, collect indications and produce evidence. He too must not resign himself to hypotheses, half-truths or partial truths. In any case - even on big questions - there is only one truth! There cannot be more than one truth! That would be a contradiction. There is only one correct answer to all questions and therefore only one truth. The whole truth or the sum of all truths is composed of many individual parts or fragments, similar to a puzzle. Putting the whole game together is a high art!

"Anderson's fairy tale, *The Ice Queen,* says: "The mirror of truth broke a part long time ago. The shards were scattered all over the world. Every splinter of glass is a part of the truth".

Our task, Eno, is to search and pick up the shard pieces and put the mirror of the truth back together. In Herrmann Hesse's book, *The Glass Bead Game*, it also deals with this topic."

"Have you found the shards of glass, Swami, and have you put the mirror of truth back together properly?"

"Not quite yet, I'm still missing a few smaller pieces. However, I can see a large part of the truth."

"Where and how shall I seek the truth, Swami? It's not like it is just lying around everywhere."

"You can find pieces of the truth everywhere, Eno. You just have to want to see it, be open to it. The whole thing is far less complicated and difficult than you think. If you occupy yourself with it for a while, a momentum of its own develops. You learn to analyze, differentiate, connect and combine in order to put the mirror together correctly. One part makes the other."

The Swami scrutinized me with narrowed eyes.

"Eno, you look like you have traveled pretty far in the world?"

"I guess you could say that, Swami, I lived in America for a year and in Berlin for a year, traveled all over Asia and South America. All India travels added up, I spent two years in this country. I have experienced and gone through a lot on these trips. I didn't just go there on vacation or holiday."

"Wow", the Swami marveled, "that's all kinds of stuff, I suspected it, I saw it in to you. It seems to me that you are the explorer, adventurer and discover type. What are your next plans, Eno, what are your next plans for the near future?"

"Hm...I don't know yet, everything is still open, at the moment I don't have any big plans. I want to winter over here in India, enjoy life and have a great time. Later, when the weather is warmer in the north, I might travel to Rishikesh with my friend Angelo. In any case, I look for a room or a house close to the beach, the Amala-Lodge is simply too central, too expensive and too loud. I'll see what I can do after that."

The Swami was silent for a while and then said, "Eno, not only the outer world exists, there is also an inner world, a spiritual world. You have travelled a large part of the outer world but you have not yet discovered so much of the inner, spiritual world. Don't you have time and desire to discover, explore and travel the undiscovered continents of your spiritual world?

I, Swami Sathyanandapuri, I'm one of the best tour guides on this goddamn planet! I'll make you a suggestion. Why don't you move here with me under this tree, there's enough space for both of us? This tree is the most exclusive natural beach bungalow in the world. On the rice field over there is an electric pump for irrigation, you can wash and shower there, the toilet is back there in the woods. You can get food in the village at the road above - what more do you want? However, you should only bring the bare essentials of clothes and personal belongings. The fishermen are so poor, they'll steal even your old toothbrush or the last bar of soap if they have to...however, nothing has come away for a long time now. In the beginning, the first time here, it was bad, they even stole an old pair of panties from Lisa which she had hung on a branch to dry. Then the cremator put his foot down and told the fishermen to stop and fuck off. Since then I have had my peace."

"What kind of cremator?", I wanted to know.

"I'll tell you another time, Eno, what do you think of my proposal?"

"Hm...I don't really know...but why not. I wanted to move anyway - it is going well with Angelo, we are not obliged to each other. We travel sometimes together, sometimes separately. Everyone has his own goals and wishes. He wants to go to Cape Comorin and lather see the Guru Sai Baba. I'm not really in the mood for those places that anyway... okay, Swami, I accept your proposal. My hotel is paid for until tomorrow, so I'll move in the day after tomorrow if that's okay with you."

"Come whenever you want, Eno, you're welcome here anytime."

After my visit I cycled back to Pondicherry, drove straight to the Park-Hotel, hoping to meet Angelo there. I was lucky. He was sitting on the hotel veranda reading a book.

"Hello Angelo, you old Yogi", I greeted him, "I was just meeting this old Swami under the tree. Man, I'm telling you, this guy's on fire, man. I've never met anyone like him before. I always thought octogenarians are senile, calcified and conservative. Imagine, the old man invited me to stay with him under the tree for a while...I accepted! I wanted to move to the beach anyway."

"You see, Eno, I told you right away, your encounter with that Shaman-Swami under your old love tree is a special sign. This is certainly no coincidence! I think it's a great idea to move there. For my part I will travel to Cape Comorin in a week or two, from there up to Karnataka to see Sai Baba and then I come back to Pondicherry, I like it here. We can meet here again in two months and then travel north together to Rishikesh."

"Done, let's do it! You must come and visit the Swami and me before you leave."

With a ballpoint pen I drew the position of our tree on a table serviette. Chatting in the shade, we spent the rest of the afternoon on the hotel veranda and had a Palak Panier for dinner at the Aristo-Restaurant.

The next day I checked out of the Amala-Lodge. I put my luggage in the lock room for an indefinite period for a fee.

Only with one pair of trousers, three t-shirts, a few cotton cloths, sandals, raffia mat, blanket and a handful of toiletries I moved to the Swami under the tree.

"Eno, hello...there you are - welcome aboard our spaceship," he greeted me. "I see you didn't bring much with you, that's very good! The less you own, the more free you are - possession is ballast! We can't take anything at the end anyway. As you know, the last shirt has no pockets. So, it does no harm to practice letting go for some time when we are still alive."

I rolled out my raffia mat on the sandy ground in the back of the tree room, laid my blanket on it and hung the cotton bag with my belongings on a branch. I secretly buried my passport, cash dollars and the return ticket in a plastic box, I had taken along especially for this purpose, when the Swami was going to the toilet in the sand under the tree. I trusted the Swami - but safe is safe. I had met many weird birds, freaks and stranded existences on my travels in India. The burial also had the advantage that I did not have to carry the valuables on me all the time and pay attention to them.

The Swami himself lived absolutely spartanly, he had practically nothing. His clothes consisted of some string-thongs and scarfs. He also had a blanket, a kerosene lamp, a flashlight, some dinnerware, three books, writing utensils, a few sheets of paper and a shoulder bag with all kinds of bits and pieces in it.

Our tree stood on a beautiful palm tree covered area. Two hundred yards in front of us glittered the turquoise blue sea. A few steps to the side stretched a small rice field in fluorescent spring green. Not far, on the other side, you could see a small grove. To the village of Kottakuppam, on the main road it was a half mile, along a footpath, passing a draw well and two small farmhouses. On the main road in the village there were three small food stalls where you could get simple Indian meals. There was also a kind of kiosk that sold everything from string to candy and a fruit and vegetables stand - what more could I want? It was all there!

In the afternoon I enjoyed an extensive bathing, swimming, splashing and body surfing in the sea. Afterwards I tested the electric water pump shower in the rice field. From a pipe as thick as an arm the cool water clapped against me in a fountain - what luxury in India. I've never had a nicer shower in my live. To crown it all, I drank a big green drinking coconut under our tree.

"Hey, Swami, I haven't felt this good for a long time. I think it's fantastic here."

"There's one thing you're missing", the Swami interjected, "and that is a beautiful lady in a sexy bikini."

"I hadn't thought of that at all at the moment but now that you've got me on it, I have to admit that this wouldn't be not bad, of course - I'm not a disdainful of fine food! Caroline, the Australian girl I was here with, a few years ago, looked super sexy, man! When I think about it... We had a wonderful time under this tree, full of ecstasy and beauty! We swam in the sea like dolphins, in the night we made love under this tree like a pair of gods. Caroline was an incredibly great woman, once we had even made love in the Taj Mahal."

"You mean, you had sex at the Taj Mahal...?!"

"Sex, in this case, is too cheaply expressed, Swami, it was one dimension more."

"Wow!" marveled the Swami. "That sounds fabulous, go on, tell me about it...I'm curious as a feather."

"So...after six bumpy hours by bus coming from New-Delhi, we reached in the evening the city of Agra where the famous Taj Mahal is located. It was already dark. We checked into a hotel and had a snack in a nearby restaurant. Caroline insisted going to the Taj Mahal in this night. Because I had assumed that we would not visit the Taj until tomorrow in daylight, I was a little surprised and skeptic about this idea, showed not a great desire...But I let myself be persuaded - women just...? We got our flashlight from the hotel room. Because it was a bit chilly outside, Caroline put a blanket over her shoulder. At the hotel reception we asked where to find the Taj."

"A half mile up the road, you are heading straight for it."

There were hardly any people on the very sparsely lit road. After a few hundred yards there was no lighting at all and no more houses. Only the moon and the stars gave a little light. Obviously, we had reached the edge of the city. We switched on our flashlights and walked on slowly. Not a soul was to be seen, only a few goats nearby were bleating lonely through the night.

Suddenly...wham... in front of us we saw a huge, majestic, black silhouette, rising from the starry sky...the Taj Mahal - the mausoleum of eternal love!

Slowly, along a fountain basin we moved towards it. No security, no guards, no tourists, no visitors. We were completely alone! We walked through the main portal and entered the crypt where the emperor and his wife are buried. In the center stood side by side the two sarcophagi of the imperial couple. The silent, grace, beauty and grandeur of this crypt touched and moved us deeply.

Afterwards we strolled carefully through the corridors and galleries. Our weak flashlights could hardly illuminate the huge dimensions of the Taj Mahal. On one of the balconies on the second floor we sat down on Caterina's blanket...we smoked a joint and enjoyed the peace, silence and the view to the starry sky.

After a while Caroline gently put a hand around my neck and gave me a long, deep kiss... the way women do when they have more in their mind...I hadn't thought of this idea - she was ahead of me - but why not? The Taj Mahal is not a church! It is the mausoleum of eternal love! I allayed my doubts and gave myself in to love...it was intoxicating!

Imagine that we were inside the most famous landmark and monument of India, in one of the most important and beautiful buildings in the world...In the mausoleum of eternal love.

Our love adventure in the Taj Mahal was absolutely magical, ecstatic and beautiful. This unique location, this unique experience inspired us both.

To finish off we smoked a joint once more, afterwards we made our way back to the hotel. The next morning, we visited our Taj Mahal again in daylight. It was a completely different atmosphere compared to the night. Hundreds of visitors and Western tourists strolled or stood around. On our balcony, we couldn't help but smile quietly... If all those people would know...?

(Nowadays our story would not be possible anymore. The Taj Mahal is lit brightly at night by huge floodlights and monitored for twenty-four hours. The areal is surrounded by a six foot high iron fence. At the entrance each visitor has to pass through a metal detector).

The Swami found my story very amusing and was visibly impressed.

"How long has it been since you and Caroline were under that tree," he wanted to know

"Hm...wait a minute - that must be seven years ago now, it was also the end of January at that time. I'd say it was exactly seven years ago almost to the day."

"What do you think this accuracy means to you?" he asked further.

"I don't know, Swami. I would say that it was a coincidence."

"Eno, you know who means and believes - namely those who do not know! Coincidence, you mean? I don't believe it! The PC generation still believes in the Darwinian doctrine of coincidence. Yeah, you think the world just was created by fortune accident? I can assure you, the world was planned, designed, created and programmed.

You think the sun just has by coincidence exactly the right distance to Earth, huh? I can tell you, measured by the trillions of miles of infinity, the sun was hung up with damned accuracy - to the inch. A few miles closer and we would have 200 degrees in the shade, a few miles further we would freeze our asses off.

There is no coincidence, everything has its rule and law. Nothing happens purely by coincidence, everything has its reason, its intention. There are rules and order to chaos!

These apparent coincidences are precisely timed parallelisms that meet synchronously in time. These random events and happenings contain a message and information, you should ask yourself why and how come this coincidence happen to me? Why does something fall to me? Coincidence is conspicuous - otherwise it would not be conspicuous at all - it would not be noticed, it would be a meaningless event.

And if you now still think that you were here seven years ago purely by coincidence and now, exactly seven years later, you are here again by coincidence, you meet me by coincidence and I meet you by coincidence just because we both have nothing better to do - you are wrong.

When several coincidences meet, one speaks of a chain of coincidences. I received a letter from my brother exactly seven years ago at the end of January. In this letter he wrote that I am a stranded, crazy, stupid hippie, a welfare case - he had been a simple, uptight civil servant all his life and had to let out his frustration on me. This letter has hurt me deeply...

Exactly one day after this sad letter Lisa and I met at the Shiva Temple. She in turn received a letter on the same day from her father, a millionaire American Jew, informing her that he would refuse her all alimony payments in the future and disinherit her because she had converted to Hinduism as a Jew and would live as an American in an uncivilized country like India."

"It's a strange thing Swami. The day before I met Caroline, I received a mail from my girlfriend at this time - she had fallen in love with another guy and dumped me. - All these events took place exactly seven years ago - what does all this mean?"

The Swami thought concentrated for a while.

"Eno, I got it." He slapped his thigh, looked around as if someone was watching us. "Eno", he said quietly", I know now why I have been sitting under this tree for ten months, I have been waiting for you and you have been looking for me, it is like this and it doesn't make no difference!"

"Hm...if that's your conclusion, Swami, then I'm glad I found you. What do you think is the purpose of this meeting?"

"That, Eno, you will learn and find out under this tree!"

In the meantime, it had become evening, my stomach was slowly rumbling. Since breakfast I had not eaten anything except two bananas.

"Swami, I'm going up to the village to one of those food stalls. Would you like to come with me or shall I bring you something?"

"I think I'll stay here this evening. I rarely eat dinner. But you could bring me a coffee, in the thermos pot and some coco-cookies."

I went to the village, there I sat down in the *Delight* food stable. These food stables are tiny restaurants the size of garages which can be seen all over India, they have seats for about eight to ten people. The furniture is small and simple. Out of the *Delight's* a fully turned up radio was buzzing with the sound of Hindi pop. On the lower ceiling a fan whirred at highest speed. I ordered a classic Indian *thali*, which was served on a large green banana leaf. The *thali* tasted excellent. The cook was pleased and offered me a betelnut pan for dessert which I shoved behind my cheek and chewed with relish. At the end I let the thermos flask I had brought with me refilled with coffee, bought a baggie of coco-cookies and paid the bill.

"You are ei frieeend good of thys old man Swami?", asked the cook.

"Yes, I'm a friend of the Swami."

"Swami it is good, holy man. I am very happy of. What is your country please?" he asked.

"I come from Switzerland."

"Oh, Swiesserland is much rich country. India is poor. What is your name please?"

"My name is Eno, and what's yours?"

"My name it is Amukaram."

"Nice to meet you, Amukaram, you're the best cook in India, see you next time, good night."

"Good night, thank you much, Sir," he replied radiantly smiling.

Back under the tree, in the light of the kerosene lamp we enjoyed the coffee and coco-cookies A little later I wished the Swami a good night and rolled into my blanket - my first open air night under the tree. The Swami browsed a little in one of his books while I let the distant sound of the waves lull me to sleep.

When I woke up the sun was dark orange just above sea level. I had slept very well, much better than in the stuffy, noisy Amala-Lodge on the much too short bed. I felt like a newborn.

The Swami was already awake. He sat meditating in lotus position on his raffia mat. I tried to match him by crossing my legs and closing my eyes.

"Concentrate only on your breath", he said after a while," breathe deeply, slowly and consciously, switch off all your thoughts."

I acted as if I was told - after a few minutes a floating lightness came over me. For a few moments I melted with my breath and heartbeat. After the meditation the Swami did some Yoga exercises. I tried to imitate them as well.

"Follow my breathing rhythm", he said, "breathing is the most important thing in yoga. Think and direct your breath to the place where it pulls and hurts. Try to raise the position slightly each time you inhale and relax it slightly when you exhale. Feel into your body and become one with it."

We practiced yoga exercises for about half an hour. Compared to the Swami I felt like an old man. His mobility and elasticity were amazing! Every muscle, every tendon was hurting me. The exercises showed their effect...after that I felt physically and freshly aligned.

"Eno, I'm going up to the street to get us some breakfast. You like *Idlis* with coconut chutney?"

"Sure, man, it's my favorite Indian breakfast!"

When I came back from my morning toilet which took place in the woods and under the water pump, the Swami was just about to distribute the *Idlis* and the chutney from a pot onto our plates. In addition, there was fresh coffee from the refilled thermos flask.

What an enjoyment, this breakfast! The *Idlis* were exactly as they should be, the coconut chutney was exactly my taste, the coffee exactly as I loved it.

"Swami, you're a genius, a true artist of life!"

"Why do you think so?"

"Just because you have nothing and nevertheless you have everything! You love a beautiful woman, you live in a beach house, you live your vocation, you are content, happy and healthy...and you possess wisdom, peace and inner richness."

"For that, my friend", replied the Swami, "I have worked very long and hard on it, giving up a lot - that was my kind of career! I would not change for anything in the world with one of those millionaires or billionaires. Do they radiate happiness, contentment, serenity? They should actually go through this world laughing and happy - but no, they are not! And why not? Because they're greedy addicts who need more and more stuff. Addicts are never happy and calm, and if they are, then only for very brief moments until the next shot or million is in...but the effects wear off very quickly.

Why are there so many heroin, cocaine, tobacco, TV, psychotropic drugs, food and alcohol addicts? I can tell you why: Because everyone runs away from himself - in his own way. And why does everyone run away from himself? Because there is an inner emptiness - the emptiness of inner values! We try to compensate this inner emptiness with all kinds of drugs and external values, which of course does not work. Against this frustration we take and need all kinds of drugs that promise us an illusion of happiness or we create artificial illusory worlds like TV. I like good films but good films are very rare. A good film you remember for the rest of your live. The trash they show on TV you have forgotten the next day – it is brainwash for the masses...and because of the brainwashed masses this planet goes downhill...but it was always like that, the masses are brainwashed by religion and political leaders!

Most people are searching in the wrong place and find nothing, then there are those who got caught on false gurus and prophets. They are lost in a dead-end street! They are even poorer off than those who have found nothing. And finally, we have the conspiracy theorists and esoteric freaks which are completely confused.

"Do you believe in God, Swami?" I asked.

"Did you say "believe", Eno? No, I do not believe in anything. The ignorant limit themselves to believe - the wise know! I can believe in ghosts, in fake news or Easter bunnies. I can theoretically believe in any nonsense. It just depends on how naive I am. I can believe in God. I can suspect him or know that he exists. Remember our detective, Eno, where would he go with only believing?

A thousand years ago, people believed that the earth was flat. On the basis of some evidence, some daring sailors and astrologers suspected it could also be a ball. A small elite of scholars, astronomers and wise men who were ahead of their time, had even more evidences and indications - they knew that the earth is a spinning ball. Galileo Galilei was one of them, he paid for this knowledge at the stake – the Catholic church did not want to accept his knowledge.

Among the believers, they are the most fanatic. Their blind faith in a religion or an ideology has already cost a lot of blood and tears! Yet ideology is only an idea, a supposedly logical idea. Even if an idea seems logical - an idea is just an idea! And religion is a memory of someone's ideas or relics - no more and no less!

Eno, you asked me if I believed in God? I can assure you I know he exists, that he is real. He or she is an infinite creative force that permeates everything. This creative power is present and throughout the whole universe - it is the "Great Spirit". Who else has created, designed and programmed the whole micro and macrocosm? That could only have been a mega super intelligence like the Great Spirit! Chance and coincidence alone would never be capable of this!"

"How must I imagine the Great Spirit to be, Swami?"

"The Great Spirit is the entire consciousness of all souls of this world, including the entire consciousness of all souls of the other worlds of the entire universe. The united consciousness of all souls of the whole universe, that is the Great Spirit!"

"Wow, Swami, this was the very best statement, the best definition of God I ever have heard!!!

I feel so honored and gifted to be with you under this tree."

In the branches of the tree I discovered a trident when my eyes wandered upwards.

"Wow, Swami, what do you need that trident for?" I marveled.

The Swami brought out the trident and showed it to me. The fork was forged from solid iron and mounted on a six feet long shaft made of polished wood. The end of the shaft formed an iron point so that the trident could be stuck into the ground.

"This is Shiva's trident," said the Swami, "I got it as a gift from my teacher in Almora twenty years ago, hand forged."

"And what do you need that thing for?" I wanted to know.

"In defence of black demons, black magicians and also when Lisa is here - you never know ...when the fishermen have drunk too much *Arrak*...I'm not the youngest anymore!"

"What is the difference between white magic and black magic, Swami?"

"White magic is the power of love, black magic is the power of hate. Love and hate are close together, like laughing and crying. Love and hate are tremendous energies which have their seat in the heart. Love opens the heart, hate hardens it. They don't say for nothing - heartless or a heart of stone. Pay attention next time for once if you hate where you feel this energy. I bet you can really feel your heart contracting. With love the opposite is true, the heart opens.

Gandhi, for example, was a white magician, Hitler a black magician. Both died a violent death. Gandhi was shot in the middle of public by a hating Hindu faith fanatic. Hitler cowardly crept in his bunker and in the end, he executed himself.

Gandhi's death was that of a hero. The whole world has grieved and paid respect to this man. Hitler's death was that of a cowardly dog. The whole world was redeemed and relieved when he died - hate destroys and ultimately always judges itself. Hitler's hatred destroyed the lives of millions of people of opposing ideologies and religions. Gandhi's love has united millions of people of opposing ideologies and religions!"

In the evening, I had just snuggled into my blanket and was still ruminating a little, while the Swami was writing a letter to Lisa - the tree of Knowledge spontaneously came to my mind.

"You know what, Swami, our tree is not an ordinary tree, it's the Tree of Knowledge."

"Like in the Bible, Eno, our tree is also guarded by a serpent!"

"What do you mean, Swami?"

"Well, as I say", he replied, pointing to a heap of brushwood lying in the undergrowth. Half of the brushwood was towards us and the other half was outside the tree, at the edge of the room, where the branches touched the ground.

"It sleeps every night under this heap of brushwood. During the day she hunts for mice, rats and frogs in the rice field."

"Oh man, Swami, you're a funny fellow, are you kidding? Are you trying to scare me, test me? Why are you telling me this just now, when I'm just snuggled up so nicely and want to drift off - why didn't you tell me this yesterday?"

"I just didn't think about it, it just came in to my mind."

"You may be crazy, Swami – just came in to my mind!? And what kind of snake is that? - Surely the most poisonous there is - a black mamba or something like that."

"No, it's a king cobra!"

"A king cobra...Swami, you're really total crazy! Just thinking about last night, I slept five steps away from a king cobra! I can't believe it! And how long is this beast?"

"Calm down, Eno...it's about seven feet long, it is absolutely harmless. If you leave the pile of brushwood in silence there is definitely no danger. I'm the still living proof."

"Still alive is good, Swami, I can't get a wink of sleep knowing there's a cobra in that pile. I have a snake phobia, the total horror of these beasts, you know? I think I'm going down to the beach to crash... by the way, there's a tarantula hanging over your head!"

"Ha-ha-ha...there are no tarantulas in India", the Swami returned.

I rolled up my raffia mat and the blanket.

"Good night, Swami, sleep tight - maybe the cobra will look for a little nest warmth and crawl under the blanket to you."

I went to the beach and chose a small sand pit to sleep in.

"Oh shit, Swami, really - that will be a real nightmare.", I thought. "a wild cobra as a pet?!"

I slept pretty badly on the beach. It was windy, damp and cold. In the morning I was accordingly clammy and tired. Before sunrise I went back under the tree. The Swami was already sitting meditating on his mat.

"Shh..." he made softly, holding his finger in front of his mouth, "I guess in a few minutes it'll crawl out of the brushwood."

I sat down next to the Swami. We waited in silence. Suddenly...after a few minutes - I held my breath - I saw a huge king cobra, about seven feet long, slowly wriggling out of the pile of brushwood and disappearing towards the rice field.

As if in trance I followed the scene. The pictures glided, past me in slow motion. When the spell was over, the tension released, I shivered slightly, was repulsed and fascinated at the same time.

"That's the magic of the king cobra", said the Swami, "Their poison has a similar hallucinogenic effect as LSD or Mescaline, with the difference that you don't survive the trip."

"I really don't need that, Swami."

"You can rest assured, Eno, it's gone all day now, she won't be home until late in the evening. The women who work in the rice field are much more vulnerable there. The Cobra is hunting, lurking there well camouflaged. If she's surprised, she can snap. In India a few hundred people die every year from cobra bites - mostly field workers.

In our case it's different, we know exactly where it is. If we leave the pile of brushwood in peace, it'll leave us in peace, too. I respect its space, it respects mine. Up to now, it has only been towards to us once, that was on the third day after I moved in here. Suddenly - I was eating a banana – it was lying there! I didn't make a sound or move, didn't dare to chew for a few minutes...the banana in my hand slowly turned brown. For over a half hour we watched each other, nobody made a move.

The Cobra was on the run - a farmer on the small embankment over there has burnt the scrawny grass and the thorny bushes. The Cobra lived there and had to flee because of the fire.

On the same day I was also on the run and ended up under that tree."

"What and from who were you running from, Swami, you're not even afraid of cobras?"

"That's how it was", he began, "before I moved under this tree, I lived in a small hut, in the garden of an Australian resident here. The Australian lived in a beautiful house surrounded by a large garden in which all kinds of plants and flowers grew. There was a small pond with goldfish, two parrots were fluttering around – briefly speaking, it was like paradise...until after a few months I found out that this Australian is a sick pedophile who lives in India for only one reason - to satisfy his damaged, broken sexuality! - In the West, these creatures are being pursued more and more persistently. In Thailand and Sri Lanka the government has tightened the laws. Unfortunately, this scum is coming more and more to India - it is like insidious poison!

Then one morning, after I found out what was going on, I confronted this bastard while he was making out with a ten-year-old boy who was sitting in a chair, distraught. I pushed this guy with my trident into the corner of the room and pressed it against his neck so

31

that the middle point of the trident was resting on his collarbone just below his throat. I looked the bastard in the eyes and told him my tough opinion, always with the pressure of the tip - this coward was trembling and begging for his miserable life - I would have loved most to spear this dog to the wall.

Afterwards I opened the drawers of his bedside cabinet with a jerk and found, as expected, these sad child porn photos and videos. I picked up the cabinet and threw the whole thing right through the glass, in a high arch out the window. It cracked and splintered. The furniture burst on the floor in front of the house. I got the kerosene canister from the kitchen, emptied the content over it, lit a match and...poof - there was a bang! The cabinet and all the disgusting dirt were burning brightly - my dreadlock beard was a bit singed, but I didn't give a damn. I went to my hut, packed my bundle, after five minutes I was gone! Angry and upset, I walked along the beach. I reproached myself severely, that I had not noticed anything for so long, that I had been so silly and naive-eyed... at some point I turned inland. I wanted to go back up to the road – And... there he stood in front of me. I had never seen such a big and beautiful cashew nut tree before!

Then I entered the dome under this tree for the first time. I was immediately thrilled, the beauty, peace and charisma of this room captivated me, I knew I would stay here for a while."

"Hey Swami, I'm going to swim, you want to join me?"

"I was just thinking the same thing, come on, let's go."

We went down to the beach, dived into the sea. I showed old Swami how to bodysurf. We had a great time, roared and cheered like children. The Swami looked simply funny with his wet dreadlocks. Bodysurfing was new to him, after a while he mastered it quite well, never wanted to stop. His small, light body was slithering over the water like a slate stone. Once when we were about to jump, a huge wave suddenly came towards us, I don't know from where. I was just about to shout: "Swami, don't jump - too big!"But the Swami was already washed away. For an anxious while I saw nothing more of him until finally his head emerged from the white spray. "Wow, what a breaker!", he cried. "It nearly knocked my old bones out of their joint sockets. I think I've had enough for today."

After the shower under the pump in the rice field, again under the tree, we shared a papaya and drank coconut milk with it.

"Do you really believe in an apocalypse or an end of the world?" I asked him.

"Like I said, you can leave the believing to the fools. I'm not one of those "apocalypters". The world as such has existed for a long time and will continue to exist for a long time. But the people will have to pay a high price for ignoring the laws of the world and of nature...wars, epidemics, hunger, natural disasters, poisoning and radiation will take away large parts of mankind. There are painful, dark, confused times ahead of us, worse than in the Middle Ages."

"Well, it's a bleak outlook, Swami, and nothing can be done about it?"

"Unfortunately, hardly not, mankind is still young, it corresponds to a child who only becomes wise through harm. The humanity simply has no feeling, no empathy for the dimensions of this planet. In their limitedness people think that the earth is infinite. But our world is very small - the circumference of the earth is twenty-five thousand miles, that's about twenty-five times from London to Rome or for our American friends twenty-five times from Washington to Miami. That's not so much! The layer of breathable air, that we are so screwing up is more or less three miles thick. All together, these are very small dimensions!"

In the Holy Bible it is written, "Make the earth subservient and increase you", this arrogant and pretentious thinking brought our planet and ourselves to the gums, to the edge!!! Even to a subservient or a slave we have to take care otherwise he's dying...In our case we can't buy another one. To make it clear...If we do not care for our Earth, this Earth will die and mankind too...and the future is...in two hundred years our planet looks like the Mars."

"Do you know this joke, Swami?... Two planets meet in the space:

"Hello, old friend, nice to see you again, how are you?"

Hello, buddy, thanks for asking, well I am not good at all, I'm seriously ill. I have homo sapiens!'

"Oh, I'm so sorry for you, I had that once as well, but don't worry, it will pass away."

"Cool joke, Eno, I like this kind of extraterrestrial black humor!"

If the Great Spirit really exists, Swami, this creator, why doesn't he end up war and terror?"

"I can tell you why, Eno, if the Great Spirit ended the war today, we would continue the same one tomorrow or start another one! The Great Spirit wants us to become conscious. That we end the war ourselves - that we don't even start it."

In the evening, before going to bed, I was quite paranoid about the Cobra, so I rolled out my mat as far as possible from the pile of brushwood. The Swami, in case, was closer to it than me, so that calmed me down a little...

"Good night, Swami, you, old snake charmer! I'll take a chance - if I'm dead tomorrow, I'll leave you my belongings?"

"All right, Eno, you old scared bunny. Did you know - cobras love bunnies, they like especially scared bunnies.

"Hey, old Swami, good morning...Wow...I'm still alive! Today is Sunday, I'm going to get us a good breakfast from the village, are you with me?"

"Good idea, Eno, I'll practice some Yoga in the meantime."

I went to the village where I had fresh coffee filled up at Amukaram's, bought *Puris, Idlis* and a Papaya.

When I came back to the tree, the Swami was in handstand.

"Eno, look - I lift the whole world!" he shouted.

I had to laugh...I had never heard of such an interpretation of the handstand.

After breakfast, the Swami dug a red clay *shilom* out of his bag and stuffed it with ganja. "Every Sunday I smoke a Ganja *shilom* in honor of Shiva...bum Shiva!"

We alternately inhaled the smoke, blew it in all four directions and thanked the four elements: Earth, water, air and fire.

"Hey, Swami, old red skin, in my youth I read a lot of Karl May books – the American Indians always puffed *Kinikinik* there."

"Yes, yes...the old American Indians...those were the days," mused the Swami, "what would have become of them if the white man had never discovered or settled America? Maybe they would have invented the wheel by now and still smoke *Kinikinik*. I like Karl May, he had a high ethics and respect for every culture."

"Swami, I feel like having a Sunday roast and a bottle of *Beaujolais*", I joked, "after thirty years in India, I'm sure that would be a palate joy, don't you think so?"

"You know what I would do with that Sunday-antibiotic- hormone- roast? I would throw it back there in the sand - of course I eat vegetarian as a Swami, once a week I eat a fish dish. A bottle of *Beaujolais*, however, I would not despise. I haven't had a sip of alcohol for the last twenty years. Drinking together with you an old, good bottle wine, I would make an exception."

One morning after meditation, Yoga and breakfast, I sat down in front of our tree in the shade facing the sea and read the *Times of India* which I had bought at the kiosk in the village. Crackling noises, quiet steps made me lift my head and look up.

A few yards in front of me stood a young Indian woman of about twenty years. She wore a fluorescent, bright red sari of a luminosity that only Indian fabrics and colors can achieve in Indian sunlight. I was really dazzled and held my hand in front of my eyes as if to protect myself from the sun. Her lips shone in the same bright red to match her dress, with a contrast of chestnut brown, delicate skin, framed by black, shiny, long hair, combed backwards in the Indian style. For one sequence our eyes met...she nodded shyly in greeting and smiled briefly. Such white teeth, such brown doe eyes, the little sapphire on the nostril, this incredible figure - I was left speechless! - This young woman would be the crowning glory of any beauty contest.

The beauty was carrying a wicker basket and was collecting brushwood. She did her round around our tree without touching the cobra's brushwood pile.

"Hey, Swami, did you just see that woman in the red dress collecting brushwood?"

"You like her, don't you?", he stated. "This is the eldest daughter of the farmer who tills the rice field."

"Such a beautiful daughter he has", I wondered how he did it. The farmer himself looked more like a small, humpy gnome.

"Our farmer has not only one daughter, but three of them, all beautiful, of marriageable age. He has no sons. With three daughters, this poor peasant is punished for the rest of his life! I don't want to wear his yoke, that's why he has such a hump."

"Can't understand, Swami, one isn't punished with such beautiful daughters."

"The problem is", the Swami continued, "the farmer has to pay at least 50,000 Rupees dowry for each daughter if he wants to marry them well. With three daughters, that is 150,000 Rupees, a sum that our little farmer is almost unable to raise. The peasant family barely has enough to survive. The small rice field, the two cows and the four goats don't give much, how can the old man scratch together 150.000 Rupees - almost impossible!

And for this reason, Eno, many girl babies of these poor fishing and farming families are killed after birth! They are suffocated with a pillow or put to sleep with opium...in that little grove there, those little girl souls are buried."

"Oh, wow... Swami, that's incredible! That's horrible! Is it really true what you're telling me?"

"Unfortunately, it is the bitter truth! The very poor families often have no other choice. Their argument is that it is better to have only four heads which are more or less fed up, than to have six heads which are always half hungry, and cost dowries. The Indian middle class solves the problem differently - in recent years, ultrasound tests have become very fashionable. It is already determined in the womb, whether its boy or a girl - the girl gets aborted! - In this respect India is merciless!

There are areas and villages, especially in the north, where there are almost no women left - it is estimated that there are 100 million women missing in India."

"Then we'd have to abolish this stupid venom system," I indignant.

"The paradox is that the government has forbidden the dowry by law but the people hold on to this centuries-old tradition.

There are also many marriage swindlers here, they collect the dowry from the bride's family and then they disappear!

The Indians are accumulating a hell of a lot of bad karma. They will have to pay for it one day!"

"What exactly is karma, Swami?"

It is the law of action and reaction - every action is followed by a reaction. Positive actions are followed by positive reactions. Negative actions are followed by negative reactions. This is the law of karma!

The rest of the day my thoughts revolved around this beautiful peasant girl whose parents have to pay a dowry to find a husband for her. I also thought of the many little girl babies buried in the woods. They were murdered because they were girls - a cost of 50,000

Rupees, which was about 1000 US dollars - Under our tree I had buried my travel money of 2000 dollars...What in turn were 2000 dollars, worth in the West? - The differences on this planet are really serious!!

For dinner we went to the *Delight* food stall, where Amukaram prepared a huge *Masala Dosa* for us. Amukaram was really a star cook, there were not even such good *Masala Dosas* in the luxury restaurant in the city. It was a delight to watch him cook. Certainly, he had prepared thousands of these *Masala Dosas* in his life, every move was right, the timing was perfect.

For dessert he offered us a kind of semolina head that was covered with a brown sauce. His little chubby son sat on Swami's lap, and from time to time he was allowed to nibble on the semolina. Finally, he licked out the plate with the rest of the sauce, he was panting with joy and his eyes were shining. The Swami with the li-ttle-one on his lap was really a nice picture. When he then pulled his long white beard, the whole food stable had to laugh. - How similar all children of this world are, later are they made Christians, Muslims, Jews or Hindus...

"Eno, can you play chess? If yes, I would like to play a game with you", the Swami asked me when we were back under the tree.

"To some extent, I haven't played for a long time - but where do we get a chess game here in the middle of the pampas?"

"This is not a problem", replied the Swami while digging a plastic bag from the sandy ground from which he took a medium-sized chess set made of carved, polished wood.

We drew our chessmen, the Swami got the white ones, I got the black ones. In addition to the kerosene lamp, the Swami placed a candle to the left and right of the chessboard. I poured fresh coffee from the re-filled thermos flask into our cups.

That evening we played four games which the Swami won in a superior way. For the Swami chess was the game of all games. He was a master of this game - Yoga for the mind, as he called it - the infinity on 64 fields.

"All life is a game, a serious game, a kind of computer game", he explained, "we are the players, the pawns. Sometimes the game is exciting, sometimes it's boring, sometimes it's funny, sometimes dramatic, as games are.

The present move, the present decision influences the whole future game, the whole future life...even more, the present decision can even turn the whole game upside down. In extreme cases, an inattention, a wrong reaction can end the game or the life! In the chess-game, as in the game of life, all future depends on the present decision. Shall I take the Rook to catch the Bishop, or maybe the Pawn to cover the Queen? Should I look for a new job or expand my position in my current company? Should I stay in London or maybe move to Manchester, with or without the Queen? The game of life constantly forces us to make new decisions that need to be well thought out and considered - because every action is followed by a reaction!

Life is not just a game of chance, nor is it as simple as *Poker* or *Black Peter*. And it's not just about the money, like in *Monopoly*, it's about much more - namely the future character in a new future game!

At the end of the game, a referee will analyze and judge the whole game. And it's not a question of whether you won or lost the game, but as what and how you played whether you followed the rules of the game and how much of the whole game you understood, you understand, Eno?"

"Somehow...I think I know what you mean, Swami. When I look at you, you seem like the white Pawn on the left outside of the field. You made one or two moves and did not intervene in the game afterwards. Instead, you let the game passing you, wondering why the game at all exists, who invented it, and what the point and meaning of the game is."

"Not so badly analyzed, Eno! I see you have a sense to the essence of the things. By the way, did you know that the game of Chess was invented 15oo years ago in India at the court of a Maharaja by a game maker. This game maker was a gifted genius, an artist who had already created dozens of board games, the Chess-Game was his life's work! The first game of Chess in this world was played by the Maharaja and the game maker. Off course the game maker let the

Maharaja win... The Maharaja was excited about this newly invented game. It was so completely different from all the others he had known before. In the evening when he was alone, he placed the wooden figures on the checkered Marble-board once again and watched the game for a long time...After a while he saw in this game, the game of all games, life itself. He saw infinity, timelessness, eternity. It became clear to him - as long as one would play this game - even if it was thousands of years - no two games would be the same! The Maharaja called this game the "King-Game". I have often wondered who is the inventor of the chess-game, the wheel or the bow. Imagine if we could now look back with a time machine - just as these crazy geniuses were making their invention - that would certainly be a mo-ving moment!

For every game there are rules that should be followed and observed, whether it be in music, cooking or the game of life - everything is a game. The slightest movement with my arm is an interaction of several muscles. Imagine if the interaction of clutch, gas and brake does not work when driving a car...

Mankind has also been given clearly defined rules for playing on this earth. Unfortunately, he does not follow any of these rules, that's why we have such a disaster on this planet!

The Ten Commandments of Moses were originally twenty-four rules of play. Unfortunately, later religious leaders reduced, manipulated and censored these universal rules of the game. They made it into commandments and prohibitions. In the bible there is the manipulated, pitiful rest which is not much helpful for us for living together on this planet. Try to play a game with half and changed rules - the game becomes headless, loses its meaning."

"Do you know these twenty-four rules?" I asked the Swami.

"Yeah, sure I know them or do you think I'm telling you things I don't know myself? We all know these rules, they are record in our collective consciousness! Deep down inside we all know what is good and what is bad!"

The Swami rummaged in his bag and took out a decorated piece of bamboo cane about then inches long which was closed at both ends with wooden plugs. From this he took a yellowed roll of rice paper, which he handed to me. Carefully I unrolled the paper and read the black, squiggly writing:

The 24 rules of the game for the humans on Terra:

    1. You should not hate.
    2. You should not envy.
    3. You should not be greedy.

4. You should not kill and murder.
5. You should not torture and plague.
6. You should not compel and rape.
7. You should not commit incest and fornication.
8. You should not abuse your power.
9. You should not rob and steal.
10. You should not lie.
11. You should not betray.
12. You should not denounce.
13. You should not intrigue.
14. You should not be a coward.
15. You should not be selfish.
16. You should not be unfair.
17. You should not despise.
18. You should not be arrogant.
19. You should not be stingy.
20. You should not get addicted.
21. You should have respect and esteem for the animal, plant and mineral kingdoms.
22. You should take care and responsability for earth, water, air and fire.
23. You should strive for wisdom, truth, knowledge, and love.
24. You should honor the great spirit and his creation.

In the name of the Great Spirit
Swami Sathyanandapuri

"Wow, Swami!" I am amazed, "did you compose and write this yourself?"

"Not quite, the "Great Spirit" helped me and dictated to me. It was like this...Twenty years ago I lived in Almora, up in the Himalayas. Once I fasted and kept silent for forty days there, in a completely remote, lonely area, never ate a bite, never spoke a word, never saw a person. It's quiet as dead up there. Not a single sound of civilization gets up there.

In that time, I came very close to the "Great Spirit". I recognized him and his creation, understood the meaning of life and the meaning of death. In the end I felt almost bodyless. I felt light as a feather, consisting almost only of spirit. During the last three days of my period of fasting, I received visions of an incredible clarity and intensity, that I had never thought is possible before! There I realized that real visions are much more than ideas, dreams, inspirations or hallucinations. Real visions are absolutely real. They are as clear as 3-D cinema, only with the difference that you find yourself in the middle of the film – in the cosmic cyberspace! But you can't choose the film yourself, it is played to you by the Great Spirit.

On the fortieth day I received cyberspace-like visions of return to past lives and I also foresaw my future and death! All of this was the hardest thing I had ever experienced, gone through and lived through in my whole life - and that after forty days of fasting and silence! Afterwards I was as exhausted and burned out like a piece of rotten wood in the desert.

And as I was sitting there, suddenly - I don't know where he came from - a Sherpa boy of about fourteen years stood in front of me. He was loaded with three thick bundles of rice paper, two bottles of black ink, a whole box of those old-fashioned steel feather spare pens and wooden holders. I assumed that the boy had bought the writing utensils in the city and was on his way to one of those Tibetan monasteries - The first human being after forty days of loneliness! For a long time, the boy looked at me without saying anything. I also said nothing. After a while he handed me two sheets of rice paper without saying a word, took a wooden holder out of the box, stuck a feather on it and poured some ink into a used disposable plastic cup he was carrying with him and laid it all down in front of me. I sat there like frozen. I knew this was no coincidence, this is a sign from the Great Spirit! I gave the Sherpa-boy twenty Rupees. He was overjoyed with it, put his palms together for goodbye, thereupon he continued on his way.

I took the pen in my hand and said aloud: "Great Spirit, I thank you with all my heart for my rich and full life. My path of life was not always easy, often it was stony, often it was dark, at last it was very steep, it led me to the Himalayas - to you! The long way was worth it to go, I got more than I ever expected, more than I ever dreamed of. Great Spirit, you sent me a Sherpa-boy who gave me paper and a pen - I hear and write down your words so that they will never be lost again!" After a while, as if by magic, my hand began to write...When the dictation was over, I put down the pen and read what I had written. Then I said, "Great Spirit, I thank you for guiding my mind, for leading my hand. I will keep and follow these rules of the game, I will make sure that they become conscious again among the people!"

I rolled up the paper, I had written on, got up and walked about two hours to the next small village, where after forty days of fasting I ate a yoghurt, some rice and a banana at a food stall."

"Wow...For forty days you have been silent and fasting in solitude", I marveled, "that's real madness, Swami, how did you bear it and survive?"

"Everything has its price," replied the Swami, "I have received quite a lot in return. Jesus, Mohammed and Buddha also fasted for a long time - why not Swami Sathyanandapuri? These people only became what they were after they had had such experiences.

The North American Indians sent the young boys into the wilderness for a certain time, where they fasted and meditated in solitude until they obtained visions. Only then they were allowed to return to their village, where they received a new name based on their vision. Only then they were accepted into the covenant of adult men."

"And in our society, Swami, they put the young lads into the army so that they can become men - One of my favorite sayings is: Imagine it's war and no one goes there!"

By the way, do you know where and how I survived Hitler and World War II? In exile - in Finland, in the endless forests byside a lonely lake...a hundred miles not a single soul, far away from any civilization. There I built myself a small log cabin, survived on fish, potatoes, mushrooms, berries and some hunting - for five lonely years, for five dark winters."

"Wow, Swami, that sounds like an absolute hardcore story...tell me."

"That's how it was", he began, "I flied away from Germany in the autumn of 1939, three days after Hitler's declaration of war on Poland. At first I went to Denmark, then via Sweden to Finland. In the spring of 1940, when the war was spreading out and I was also having difficulties with the Finnish authorities, I bought an old wooden rowing boat in Tampere and purchased fifty pounds of seed potatoes, five pounds of corn, two pounds of salt and three pounds of onion seedlings. I also bought a used hunting rifle, tools, fishing tackle, a small pharmacy, three bottles of vodka and all the tobacco I could get.

One dark night, so that no one would see me, I rowed - with two chickens and a rooster on the boat - heavily loaded...into the endless labyrinth of the thousand lakes. On the fourth day I discovered a well camouflaged, difficult to access narrow bay, surrounded by dense forest - exactly what I was looking for! Near the shore there was a forest glade where I could create a small field with relatively little effort. That was the first thing I did. I platted the glade, turned over the earth, planted the seed potatoes, the onions and sowed the corn.

After that, a rather hard time began. For weeks I lived on fish, deer, nettles and wild garlic. Finally, the summer came with its raspberries, cranberries and blueberries. In autumn I found pounds of mushrooms which I dried as many as possible for the winter. The potatoes had also grown magnificently. The onions looked good. Only the corn had become a little sparse. Even the chickens had got used to the new environment, laid an egg every now and then. I remember...just before Christmas, 1940, I bagged a big elk. On December 25th I had a juicy elk steak with fried potatoes in mushroom sauce...but the following March I had eaten the last potato and the very last corn kernel, only the seed vault were left. From then on, I ate fish, deer, nettles and wild garlic again. Every week the chickens laid a few eggs. In the second year, the harvest was bigger, and I was able to make it through.

In the winter I heard cannon thunder from afar. I assumed the Germans would attack Finland. I had no idea that it were the Russians. For a few weeks this distant, rumbling thunder continued. After that it was quiet for years...so quiet and lonely that sometimes I almost went crazy. Loneliness was my biggest adversary during these years! I often had conversations with former fellows, old friends, women who were once my lovers... sometimes the idea, the imagination, became so perfect that it almost became real, almost reality. I often wanted to put an end to my lonely wolf-life. Often, I screamed my pain into the deep, endless forest.

One day, in autumn 1945, after five years of solitary loneliness, my cries were heard. In response I heard dogs barking. A little later two Finnish hunters appeared in the undergrowth. After the initial scare and distrust on both sides - I looked like Robinson Crusoe after all these years, the situation cleared up. One of the hunters spoke some German. He explained me that the war in Europe ended in the spring, that Hitler was dead. The Finns also explained and summarized in broad outlines the course of the war, of which I had no clue. They told me about Auschwitz, about Stalingrad, about Hiroshima...my hair stood on end! Such an enormous extent of hatred, cruelty, destruction and dead human lives could not be grasped or understood by my mind in this short time. Again, and again the Finns had to assure me that all this was true. When I told them that I had fled from Hitler's war and had been living here as a hermit for five years and that they were the first people I had spoken to since then, these two quiet Finns went giddy with pleasure. They danced, cheered and patted me on the shoulder, offered me from a bottle of vodka and with it, dark bread, which I enjoyed crumbs by crumbs. After one hour the two hunters said goodbye and continued their way.

I, for my part, packed a small bundle three days later, took farewell from my birch log cabin, my little bay, got into the boat and rowed south - I was forty years old, the war was over, life laid ahead of me - I had a lot of catching up to do!"

But I have never forgotten my little birch log cabin in the deep, cool, Finnish forest where I survived the war...sometimes in midsummer, when it gets unbearably hot here, like an oven, I dream about it."

"Wow Swami, strong tobacco, an incredible story - all I can do is giving a standing ovation and pull off my hat."

"By the way, Swami, my mother is Finnish, I spent countless times my holidays with my grandparents, in a log cabin at the lake. I often went fishing there as a boy and rowed around in a wooden boat. I feel very close to this country and the people there. I even speak the language."

"You don't say", the Swami amazed, "I am very pleased that you also have a connection to Finland, that is certainly no coincidence."

We spent the rest of the evening reminiscing about old memories of Finland - After this story and both of us loving Finland I liked the Swami even more and trusted him completely.

The other morning - I was awake before the Swami - I just saw the tail of the cobra disappearing towards the rice field. I ate a banana and went down to the beach. When I dived into the waves, the first rays of the rising sun appeared above the now almost mirror-like sea. I felt super good, did a whoop out of sheer exuberance, clapped my hand on the water - what a life!

After the shower in the rice field I went to the draw well to fill our clay jug with fresh water. There I met the beautiful farmer's daughter who also fetched water.

"Good morning, Miss, how are you? You look very nice today", I greeted.

She got a little embarrassed and said, "thank you."

"May I ask your name, please?"

"My name is Shanti."

"Nice to meet you, my name is Eno, I live under that tree over there. Have a nice day", I wished her.

"You too", she replied and moved away towards the farmhouse, carrying the earthen water jug on her head.

I lowered the metal bucket on a rope down the well shaft which was about four yard's deep, let it fill up, pulled it up again and used it to fill our metal bucket, which held about two gallons. I hoisted it onto my shoulder and made my way back to the tree.

"Good morning, old Swami, did you sleep well?", I greeted him. "Hey dude, you know to who I just ran into? The farmer's daughter, Shanti is her name, I think I've fallen in love!"

The Swami stopped while yawning and stretching, swallowed empty and looked at me perplexed.

"Eno, you're crazy!" he cried, "even that! I hope you're not serious. Don't do anything stupid, this isn't the Wild West! In India, you can't just hit on a woman like you're used to. She'll only get involved with you if you have marriage plans. There's nothing going on here before the wedding anyway, you can put that right out of your mind. I don't think you'd be happy in the long run with this Indian farm girl."

"I wasn't happy either with educated office chicks from the west...but you're right, Swami - it just came over me for a moment, I'm twenty-eight years old...the hormones, you understand? Imagine, Swami, if I would marry Shanti I'll give the old Dad a couple of hundred bucks and he'll have his dowry problem off. Maybe we could buy another piece of land to his farm...we could all live happily. That would be a good way to get out of this whole stressful elbow-, career-, training- and performance-society."

"I can understand you very well", replied the Swami, "such similar thoughts led me to stay here in India thirty years ago. It is certainly not all for the best here either. On the contrary, I love this country and its people, despite all its contrasts that you are confronted with every day.

Indian society is very tolerant in its own way, very generous. You can be a storyteller, monk or ear cleaner in this country without any problems. And it does not matter whether you live in a cave, on a mountain top or under a tree. You are allowed to do the handstand at a crossroad for a week, no authority would forbid you to do it, people would show you respect - and if you do it for any god, you are almost a saint. Imagine me, living under a tree in Germany as a half-naked Swami. It's unimaginable!

Years ago, I threw my German passport into the Ganga-River which had expired long ago anyway. I have neither a passport nor a document about my identity - something like this is only possible here in India! Because I stand out as a white Swami, it happens from time to time that the police stopped me, asking me for my passport, for the tourist visa. I greet them in the Indian way, put my palms together on my forehead, look the cop in the eye and say, "I am Swami Sathyanandapuri, I am a citizen of this world and this universe. I have lived in India for thirty years. I have no papers or ID...Bum Shiva!' The cops usually accept that without any problems. Indian beggars and sadhus rarely have an identity card - why should a Western Swami carry one on him? Fortunately, they don't know that every vagabond in our country has an ID. Only once, a few years ago in New Delhi, a pig's face of a cop colonel wanted to cause stress and put me in jail. There I sat on the floor for three days meditating and fasting, reciting the *Bhagavad-Gita* and chanting *Om Shiva Om* all the time. Thereupon the cop colonel was convinced of my holiness, apologized and let me go."

One morning after breakfast..."Hey, Eno, let's do some Yoga exercises, I think we'll soon have a visit from Caterina, a healer from England. Caterina has studied acupuncture and homeopathy, has mastered various types of massage and has a degree in Reiki. She visits me twice a month and gives me a full body massage, after that I feel twenty years younger - a great woman, you have to meet her."

A few minutes after we had finished our Yoga exercises, a soft crackling in the undergrowth indicated that we had a visitor. A young woman of about twenty-five years of age with a clean-shaven head entered the inside of our tree. I inevitably had to think of the bust of Nefertiti, the beautiful Egyptian pharaoh. Caterina wore a kind of overall made of shiny, wine-red Indian cotton silk. In one hand she was holding a bamboo stick, in the other, one of those old classic leather doctor's purses. For a moment I became a little insecure - this woman had an incredibly strong charisma! The Swami introduced us to each other.

"Nice to meet you again, after so long", she greeted me.

"Likewise", I replied, although I did not know why she said, "after so long." The three of us were small-talking, fooling around a little, I soon lost my initial shyness. Caterina was absolutely warm, funny and charming. Immediately the Swami laid down on his mat. Caterina took a massage oil from her handbag and rubbed it into the Swami's back.

Meanwhile I went to the village where I went to Amukaram to buy *Idlis*, fruits and fresh coffee. Amukaram was friendly as always and in a good mood.

"Oh, Mistel Eno, how is it go? Caterina today visiting thi Swami, I already seen, Miss Caterina is doctor very good. She made my small son healthy again with special herbal Tschai."

Back under the tree the massage was still in full swing.

"It is not so easy to massage the Swami", Caterina jokingly said, "he is so thin, you literally have nothing between your fingers."

"You have to go down one floor, you have all sorts of things between your fingers there", roared the Swami.

"Be quiet, you, old lecher!", Caterina returned, patting him on the bottom. After the massage, the Swami relaxed a little while. Caterina also rested for a moment. I put the food on the plates, poured the coffee into the cups. Over dinner Caterina told us that she is currently taking lessons with an Indian Thai and kickboxing champion. I almost got the *Idli* stuck in my throat - I had never met a woman who kickboxed before!

After dinner, Caterina rolled a joint of black Nepali Hashish. Already after two puffs I could feel the effect, the Hashish was extraordinarily strong. The Swami didn't smoke.

"Hey Swami, old Indian Sioux, this Nepali *Kinikinik* is really something", I said broadly.

"I can tell by your grin and bedroom eyes", he mocked back.

"Eno, do you like to have a massage", Caterina asked me, "for a hundred Rupees I'll give you a super massage that will do you good."

"Why not, good idea, that's exactly what I need right now."

Caterina hadn't promised too much. The effect of the Hashish and the subsequent massage put me in a pleasant, gliding state. I was floating on a hundred clouds that carried me away...

When I woke up, it was already midafternoon. The Swami sat writing on his mat.

"Hello, Swami, good morning... Is Caterina no longer here? Wow, I must have dozed off during that massage. I feel like I'm born again, man, that's a real cool lady, mega cool."

"I'm supposed to say best regards to you when you wake up."

"Thank you, Swami...Is Caterina a single woman or involved in any relationship in any way?", I wanted to know.

"Ah...look at that, this morning you were in love with Shanti and now already with Caterina, but that's going very quick with you. I'm sure she would be an intere-sting match for you, at the moment, however, it is difficult to get at her. Caterina had very bad luck, she was raped half a year ago. She suffered a trauma, a shock. Her self-esteem has suffered greatly. Her trust in men is quite damaged! That's why she takes these kickboxing lessons. She's just terrified that something like this could happen again."

"Sad story…Swami, damn it, sometimes I'm ashamed to be a man."

"Hey, old Swami, I'm going for a little swim, you want to join me?"

"Another time", he waved, "I've had enough from last time."

From far away I already saw something big, weird and shiny lying on the beach.

"Strange thing", I thought, "looks like a torpedo or an airplane nozzle…but could also be an aerial bomb – But no, the thing moved slightly now. Oh…dear, a washed-up shark! Clearly, I could see the dorsal fin. Cautiously I approached - you never know…maybe suddenly the shark will flap around and bite off my leg.

Two steps ahead - is that even possibility? - the shark turned out to be a dolphin that laid helplessly in the sand and could not return to the water.

How did the dolphin get to the beach? The last high tide mark was about four yards in front of him - strange, the dolphin hadn't jumped onto the beach just like that! I saw he was very weak. Helplessly he rowed with his fins. A gasp of air came out of his breathing hole. In fast motion I remembered all the Flipper-Films I had seen on TV in my youth - the breathing hole and skin of a dolphin should always be moist - here both were completely dried out! Quickly I took off my swimming trunks, dipped them in the sea and wetted the skin and breathing hole with them. The dolphin obviously seemed to like it. Carefully I put my wet trunks around the breathing hole and sprinted back to the tree stark naked - the Swami was quite astonished.

"You look like you got a bunch of horny chicks after you."

"Forget the chicks, Swami! Down on the beach a dolphin is stranded, it is dying - we have to help it, quickly! We need one or two towels and the laundry bucket", I gasped out of breath while putting on another pair of shorts.

The Swami seemed quite perplexed... probably seldom there was so much lightning action in his peaceful life under the tree, but finally he understood. And so, we ran, me in front with the bucket, the Swami in the back with a few cloths to the beach where the dolphin was lying. The Swami dived the cloths into the sea, laid them soaking wet over the dolphin. I poured another two or three buckets of water over it.

"Wow...that's a big good-looking piece", marveled the Swami, "why it is so far back on the beach?"

The life or survival energy now slowly returned to the dolphin. He waved his fins, tried to crawl back into the sea with all his strength. He barely managed an inch in the process. The distance to the water, however, was four yards - not to be managed! As graceful and agile as the dolphin moves in the water, on land it is helpless and clumsy. We tried to grab its fins, but we couldn't because the dolphin was flapping around like mad, such a flapping dolphin fin was impossible to hold. I talked to him calmly, caressed him gently, the Swami sang softly Om...and after a while the dolphin relaxed and now let himself be grabbed by the fins without resistance. Somehow, he seemed to sense that we were not enemies, but friends who wanted to help him.

"Okay, Swami... one, two, heave ho!"

With all our strength we tried to push the dolphin back into the sea. But it was no use, we didn't get anywhere.

"Whew, Eno", puffed the Swami, "no chance, I guess the guy has over a two hundred pounds on him - he doesn't slide at all on the sand."

The dolphin also made a discouraged, resigned impression again.

"Then we have no choice but to dig a canal", I suggested. "I guess it's high tide right now, so the water is coming a little bit closer, up to the old water mark there in the sand. That would be about three yards, plus the length of the dolphin - should actually work."

With the help of coconut shell halves which we found on the beach, we dug a channel from the sea towards to the dolphin. With each wave the tide came a little closer, the channel slowly filled with water. Even the dolphin seemed to notice that. He became more restless again...The next, somewhat bigger wave brought the water almost to his head. Now we started to dig out the sand under the body. The following wave already washed around the head of the dolphin. This one chattered with joy and excitement. It could hardly wait to be in its element again! Slowly the water undercut the dolphin, washed away the sand.

"Hey, Swami, I guess a few more waves and we'll be done", I shouted.

Again we grabbed the fins, next wave...heave ho...this time, the dolphin came forward two yards with the backward suction. Once again - one...two, we pushed with all our force, the dolphin made crawling movements...we almost made it out of the channel. One more wave and our dolphin slowly slid back into the sea. With a grandiose leap it said goodbye to us, showed up once more, cackled a thank you, and then disappeared for good in the endless vastness and freedom of the sea. My eyes were wet – it's not every day that you save a dolphin as a Swiss! The Swami was also deeply moved. The whole rescue operation had made us sweat a lot, we were stuck full of sand. Under the shower in the rice field we washed and refreshed ourselves.

Neither the Swami nor I could explain conclusively how the dolphin could have got so far in to the sandy beach.

In the evening before going to bed we sat together for a while in the light of the petrol lamp, chatting about this and that. The Swami wanted to know if I had enjoyed America, how was the living over there. "It's

Saturday night, I would love to watch an American movie", he joked. "You must have some anecdotes and stories from this country?"

"What would you like to see, Swami, a comedy, drama or mystery?"

"Comedy!"

"Well, I'll tell you the comedy about how I wanted to buy a world map or an atlas in America... it was like this:

I was on a bicycle tour in South Carolina on the East Coast. In Sumter, a big city, I made a one-day stop-over. There, somehow I got the idea to get a world map. In the center of Sumter, on the main street, I entered a bookshop. There was an elderly sales-woman behind the counter. "Hello", I said, "I am looking for a world map or a world atlas, do you have anything like that in your range?'

"Yes, of course', she answered me, disappearing into the back room. I heard her climbing a ladder, heard a rummage in the paper. After a while she returned with a two feet long roll of paper, which she unrolled and showed me. On the map only the USA was shown...I thought..."Maybe she had misunderstood me", so I said, "Sorry, I'd like to get world map or atlas with all the continents and countries of the world on it, not just the USA.'

The shop assistant disappeared again in the back room, rummaged around, came back with an even bigger map. When we finally managed to unroll this impractical map together, it only showed the USA and Canada.

"What a monkey business", I thought - doesn't she really understand what I mean? So once again. "Well, ma'am, this is still not quite what I'm looking for, but we're getting closer. I am looking for a world map of the whole world, with all five continents and all countries, Australia, Europe, Africa...you understand?"

The lady rummaged again in the back room, presented me again one of these impractical rolling maps. This one seemed a little narrower, but longer. The saleswoman held the card against the wall, I unrolled it against the floor. On this copy the USA, Canada and South America were shown. I let go of the map at the bottom, it shot up like one of those carnival blowpipes - by now at the latest I should have given up, forgotten about it. But I wanted this world map - and if I had to, with a crowbar! I now looked at the saleswoman a little sharper, and adopted a more forceful tone.

"Hey, Miss, do you have a map of the world in this shop or not, with all countries on it, including Russia.'

When I named the Country *Russia*, the saleswoman's jaw dropped completely, she was looking at me, horrified - I felt as if I had asked for something forbidden. In the end, she told me that they didn't have anything like that in their range. I asked if there was a possibility somewhere else in the city to get what I wanted. The saleswoman thought for a while. "Very difficult", she said, "with a lot of luck, perhaps in the largest bookstore in town."

The store was only three blocks away on the same street. Behind the counter were two saleswomen. I had learned my lessons from the first shop and came straight to the point: "Good Morning, I am looking for a world map or world atlas with all two hundred countries and five continents of this world."

The two shop assistants looked at me as if I was asking for a road map of the Mars or Uranus. They both denied, shaking their heads - sorry...one of them already dug out another one of these impractical rolling cards, on which as always only the USA was shown.

"Is there really no way to get a world map in such a huge city?", I asked incredulously. From the next room an elderly guy appeared, whom I looked at helplessly...all three shook their heads - no chance!

I asked if there was a possibility in Columbia, the capital of South Carolina. The saleswoman looked in the phone book, called the biggest bookstore in Columbia - negative answer! - This can't be true!

Imagine, Swami, on the counter next to the cash desk there was a moon globe for 29 dollars, which you could illuminate inside, next to it was a stack of moon maps. I slowly got upset and asked: "Where the hell can I buy a world map in this country? You think the world is just America!' The salesgirls shrugged embarrassed with their shoulders, the guy looked at me as if he wanted to ask - Why the fuck do you need a world map? The saleslady called the Columbia bookstore again. They promised to take care of it and call back in a quarter of an hour.

In the meantime, I had a beer in the bar across the street.

Back in the bookstore, the salesgirls told me that the next possibility to get an atlas or a world map is in

New Orleans. Wow...this time I was the one who had his jaw dropped...New Orleans was over a thousand miles away in Louisiana, a state after the next!

Completely defeated, I left the bookstore, and out of pure frustration I had another beer in another bar. I simply could, didn't want to believe it, and understand what I had just experienced - in Switzerland the last kiosk in the back of the country offers a small pocket atlas but in the big, super America there were obviously whole states without world maps and atlases!

Inwardly I was terribly upset. I would have liked best to telephone the American president and tell him my opinion about this kind of controlled dulling and brainwashing of the people.

In Los Angeles I lived for a while with six people in a flat share. When we had visitors, they always introduced me as *the guy from Sweden*. I used to correct them and say, *from Switzerland*. After two months they still hadn't checked - for them, Sweden was the downsizing of Switzerland...After a while it didn't matter to me no more, so I was just the guy from Sweden, for them it didn't matter anyway. I could also have said that I come from *Swamiland* from the continent of *Acacia* - they wouldn't have doubted it at all."

The Swami was not an America fan at all, he went right along with my story, clapped his thighs enthusiastically, laughed and bawled, "I have always suspected that", he shouted, "that's the other America - not the unlimited, but the very limited!

In future you must tell me an American movie every Saturday night."

"Done, Swami, there will be a crime-story on the program next week."

A little later we rolled into the blankets, I dived down immediately. I wasn't afraid of the cobra anymore - on the contrary, I liked the fact that a cobra was sleeping a few yards next to me, just as tired and needed its sleep as much as I did.

The next morning, while we were having breakfast, we got a surprise visit from my friend Angelo.

"Ah, how beautiful, a real angel - be welcome!" the Swami greeted him.

"Right now, I don't feel like an angel at all, more like a complete idiot...! I have forgotten my passport and most of the money in a rickshaw on the bench, all gone! A little moment of inattention, I was overtired and stressed, that's how it happened!"

That was not good news at all on this quiet morning. I felt very sorry for my friend; this meant a lot of stress and unpleasant bureaucracy for him.

"By the way, I spent three days with Sai Baba at the ashram", Angelo said, "I couldn't stand it any longer, the energy there, the atmosphere didn't appeal to me at all. This Sai Baba seemed to me to be arrogant and decadent, I did not like him at all. One evening he actually materialized two amulets and a finger ring - simple magic tricks - and he behaved it rather clumsy. But the people believe him, they're not able to think straight and logical! I was not convinced at all by this Sai Baba and his Ashram. You have to be pretty naive to think that's a good thing. Or what do you mean, Swami?"

"I agree with you - this guy is screwing up the people! Believers are always are getting screwed, no matter what they believe in! In my time, many believed in Hitler, but only a few knew about Hitler."

"I also spent one day at Cape Comorin", Angelo continued, "a bleak, inhospitable place this southernmost tip of India. A few boulders, the sea is turbulent, the water is brown, and there is a strong wind. In short, the last days were in every aspect a total bust - I would have been smarter to stay here, but it's my own fault, I had to go to that damn cape and that silly Sai Baba - if I had only listened to my feelings and my heart and not to my mind. I knew Sai Baba and Cape Comorin wouldn't bring it but my mind wanted the proof. I will have to pay dearly for disregarding this rule but in retrospect one is always smarter!"

"And what do you intend to do now?" I asked Angelo."

"I guess I have no choice but to go up to New Delhi, to the Swiss embassy, I need a new passport or at least some kind of provisional one. I think I'll fly back to Switzerland for a while after this."

"I would say: you stay here for a few days with us under the tree and relax a little. Whether you report your passport lost a few days earlier or later doesn't make the roast any fatter", the Swami said.

The three of us spent a few wonderful days together. Angelo enjoyed every second, every wave, every breath.

On the fifth day, Angelo set off on his journey with a heavy heart - forty-eight hours by train to New Delhi, plus all the bureaucracy at the Swiss consulate and Indian immigration - that was not a fun trip!

"Angelo, I have studied you in detail the last few days - you are not wrong in your name, you are indeed an angel. An angel in human form. There are only a few people in angel form, you are one of them. You will not have an easy time. Be on your guard against your fellow men and so-called joy friends, do not trust them easily - angels are often exploited, deceived, abused! Be vigilant and watchful of the deceitfulness of people. Angelo, you have a rarely clear, pure charisma, and you look damn good...the earthly ones are full of envy, selfishness, lies and falsehood. They behave deceitfully, intriguer and nasty. Some of them are also brutal and evil. You have to be careful not to get into their swamp. Every person has his own specific charisma, is surrounded by his aura. A primitive hoodlum or rowdy just radiates the primitive hoodlum or rowdy. A good person radiates kindness of heart, peace and tolerance...you know how it is in our world, the good is often denounced and destroyed. They say he or she were just too good. That's why there's only one thing to do, you have to disguise yourself, wear a mask, a camouflage; otherwise you'll stand out too much. You do not deny yourself because of this, it is only for your own protection."

"I thank you for your advice, Swami, I will take it to my heart and try to put it into practice in my life. I'm sure I'll come back here again, maybe next year. It was super nice and instructive with both of you under that tree, I will remember that forever."

The Swami and Angelo hugged and said goodbye to each other, I also took farewell from my friend...we both had wet eyes. Somehow, I had a bad, queasy feeling, a feeling as if we were seeing each other for the last time in this life.

"Your friend Angelo is really an angel", said the Swami after Angelo had left.

"He won't have an easy time in this society... I'm less afraid for you there, you know how to play the masks, I've seen that you have a whole repertoire at your disposal. But you too must be careful - you have many envious people who envy your look, your charisma, your self-confidence, your imagination, your inner wealth and your wide horizon. They're just waiting for a weak moment, then they wipe you out!"

"If you knew how right you are. Swami! I've had to take a lot of nasty shots at this...but none of them made it – light is always stronger than the dark!!!!!!!!!!

-Light – Live - Love! In contrary there is:

-Darkness - Death - Destructiveness!"

On another day we visited a friend of the Swami, Bernard, an Anthroposophist from Germany, who lived three miles away from us in a bamboo house on stilts.

"Hello, Bernard, hello, you old petrified fossil, how are you?" the Swami greeted him jokingly. "You know what the problem is with the Anthroposophists?" he began. "You're all too spiritual, you lack ecstasy, and humor."

Bernard seemed to have great problems, he was sixty years old, divorced from his wife three years ago. His children - grown up in Waldorf schools - had failed in life. The son was heavily addicted to drugs, the daughter started a new education every year, which she gave up after a few months in frustration. Bernard reproached himself bitterly, seemed frustrated and unhappy. He wanted to end his life in India, hang himself from a tree. The Swami had literally found and saved him at the last minute. Bernard did not want to return to Germany again. He intended to spend the rest of his life in India. On the one hand he realized that his one-sided anthroposophical philosophy and ideology were probably the blame for his entire misery in life, but on the other hand he had difficulty admitting to himself, that for forty years he had built too one-sidedly on this one teaching alone. He realized that he had missed out on a lot as a result.

"You have eaten only dry rice for forty years, ignoring the fact that there are salads, sauces, vegetables, fruits, spices and desserts", the Swami explained, "your spiritual food was too one-sided, so you got deficiency symptoms. You have always referred to Rudolf Steiner in all aspects and questions of life. Depending on the situation, you hid behind Steiner, fought for him or used him as a shield. Your favorite saying was:

"Steiner said...in the end you turned into an immobile fossil a petrifaction, and wanted to kill yourself.

Real wisdom comes from within, it contains much more than Anthroposophy. Real wisdom lies in the combination of things. The secret of a refined meal lies in the combination of the ingredients - and you have convinced yourself that you only need dry rice. It's a miracle you're still alive!"

Bernhard offered us coffee and nut cake, on this occasion he took a few photos of the Swami and me, he said, we both fit well together. (I never thought at that time that one of these photos would end up on the cover of my book). I didn't get deeply involved in their discussion. I didn't understand enough about Anthroposophy. However, it was interesting to listen to them. Both were on a mental, spiritual path, seeking the truth. It seemed to me that the anthroposophical, Bernard, was rather in a narrow dead end, instead of the truth, that he had found a pile of stones while the Swami was surfing the data highway...Although almost twenty years younger, Bernard, looked older than the Swami. His charisma seemed ossified and stiff, his eyes seemed to have no brightness, his life energy was almost zero. He also smoked a lot of cigarettes. The Swami, on the other hand was bubbling with life energy, optimism and vitality. He had a sense of humor and joke, his eyes were glittering and shone. He spoke real, experienced wisdom, he did not just parrot something he had read or heard. He radiated equanimity and inner peace, even though he certainly hadn't had always an easy time in his life, having to digest many blows of fate.

"Rudolf Steiner", the Swami continued, "has described the spiritual worlds in his books, or circumscribed, like someone who wants to describe orgasm but has never experienced one himself. I can assure you; Rudolf Steiner never entered the spiritual worlds. But he had a presentiment that they must exist. Like the prophet Moses, he never entered the Promised Land himself, he was only allowed to look at it from a distance, far away!"

I felt somehow sorry for Bernard, he sat there all bent over and sad. He had never really learned to argue, to be himself. Everything he said was already pre-chewed by Rudolf Steiner and tasted rather bland. He got lost in the infinite ivory towers of Anthroposophy - neither the Swami nor I really understood what he meant...he just never got to the point, to the essence! It was exhausting to listen to him, my head was spinning. After three hours we said goodbye.

"Wow, Swami... and they think they belong to the intellectual and spiritual elite – imagination and conceiting are also an education!

"The conceiting of the conceited followers! "It doesn't matter whether you are a follower of Osho, Rudolf Steiner, or Ron Hubbard - as a pendant you are nothing more than a pendant! - You attach on to somebody. And when you attach yourself to someone, you obviously have a problem - a security problem - you can't get along on your own, you need a leader, someone to worship or adore. Those who catch a white magician had luck - otherwise you have ended up with *Scientology* or the *Kryon-Channeling*..."

Back under the tree, we took a short nap, the long walk by the sea and Bernard's anthroposophical, endless flights had tired us both. For dinner we went to Amukaram's Food stall. "Ah...di Swami comes with di Eno, want to eat well at di Amukaram - Amukaram is the much best cook man of India. Today I haveing fresh fish."

We each ordered a fish curry with a rice side dish.

"By the way, Eno, tomorrow we have full moon", the Swami told me during dinner. "I then leave with the first bus very early in the morning to Tiruvannamalai to the great Shiva temple to beg. The full moon festival lasts the whole day and the whole following night until the next morning. With the first early bus I come back again. Tomorrow is my working day, which lasts 24 hours. Would you like to join me?"

"Thanks for the invitation, Swami, actually I was planning to go to town again tomorrow to carry out some things and do some shopping. However, I could follow you on the afternoon bus."

"As you wish, Eno, you will definitely find me on the left side of the south portal, by the big tower, that's where I have my regular place."

In the evening we played another game of chess, which the Swami, of course vastly superior won in half an hour!

The Swami went to bed a little earlier than usual today, he had a busy and hard day tomorrow...

Then he left at the crack of dawn, I was still half asleep and didn't notice much. An hour after sunrise I got up too. After a shower in the rice field, I sat down for a moment on the sea side, in front of our tree.

Already from a distance I saw a woman walking along the beach in my direction, in her arms she seemed to be carrying an infant - strange! What's a woman with an infant doing on this deserted, solid part of the beach? Just below our tree she laid the child on the sandy ground. The child was wrapped in a colorful cloth, the head I could not make out, the little-one was very quiet and seemed to be sleeping. Now the woman began to dig a pit in the sand with her bare hands. In this pit she placed the child wrapped in towels. My mind was not yet ready to accept, to understand what was going on. Desperately, I searched for another explanation...but, there was no one! This mother buried her own dead child! - That was the ruthless reality! On this beautiful, calm morning, this was a brutal film cut, a stab with the dagger right into the heart! That was the brutal, merciless side of India!

The desperate mother lamented and cried bitterly. After she covered the grave, she built a small sand mount on top of it, which she decorated with seashells...it broke my heart - Where was the husband of this woman, where were the relatives, the sisters, brothers, the parents? For me, none of this was comprehensible. I was extremely restless, sad and stunned, I could hardly stand it under our tree. I wanted to go to this lonely woman. It was a great need inside me, to tell her my sorrow and sympathy. But, could I really do that, was it appropriate, what did I know about this foreign culture? In the end I was a white tourist from the West. I did not know how she would react, maybe she wanted to be alone, not be disturbed. Maybe she gets scared, throws a handful of sand in my face and runs away screaming. I didn't want to scare her. After an hour that seemed eternal to me, this poor creature was still sitting in front the grave of her child, crying and complaining. - I felt completely down! What should I do in the face of this situation? I felt that the woman had to be very thirsty - crying makes you thirsty very quickly, besides it was already around noon and very hot on the shadowless beach. I pulled myself together, only obeying my instincts and feelings. All conventions, religions, racial differences and gender differences did not give a damn to me at that moment, it was my human duty to stand by this poor person in this difficult hour. I filled a used pet bottle with water and went very carefully and slowly, right hand on the heart, to the crying woman. I nodded briefly in greeting, put my palms together and handed her the water bottle. She greedily reached for it and drank half the bottle empty. The woman was about thirty years old, from her poor clothing I concluded that she belonged to the *Dhalids*, the untouchables - the lowest level of the Indian caste system. I sat down beside her at a suitable distance. She didn't seem to mind, on the contrary, there was a brief relief on her face. She was glad not to be alone anymore, someone who took part in her fate obviously did her good. In this moment of mourning she too forgot the caste, race and gender differences. Silently and sadly we sat together in front of the small shell-decorated sand grave - There is the moment of those feelings where there are no more words needed! The only word that came over the lips of the grieving mother was *Suraya*, pointing to the grave - For that moment we were one family and Suraya was my daughter.

After half an hour I said goodbye, gave the woman a hundred Rupees and went back under our tree. There I changed my clothes, then I took the bus to Pondicherry.

During the drive I recalled this harrowing funeral. I suspected that this was just the beginning of a new cycle with the Swami under the tree. Had I known what was to come in the future, I probably wouldn't have returned.

At the Hot-Breads, a French bakery, I drank two cappuccinos and ate a chocolate croissant - a great variety after all those *Idlis!* A German Osho-Sannyasin in wine-red and orange clothes, one of these worshippers and admirer types with a Mala around his neck, took a seat at the same table - radiating an aura of the *wannabe* enlightened ones. I let myself be drawn into a short conversation, which mainly revolved around Osho, which resulted in pre-chewed statements by Osho, following everything he said - similar to Bernard the Antroposopher. On my travels in India I had often encountered Sai Baba, Amma and Osho devotees - I could never get anything done with them. Something seemed to make me fundamentally different from them! I had even read a book by Osho once, it wasn't even that bad - but therefore becoming a devotee of worship?

Afterwards I went to the GPO. A message from my parents and a heartfelt love letter from Erica had arrived in Poste-Restante. I immediately called my parents from the Telegraph-office to Switzerland. My mother told me that there were ten inches of snow at minus five degrees - and I was sweating here with the fans turning in the plus area of seventy degrees. For a moment, I was overcome by the great feeling of compassion that tropical migratory birds feel for those who stayed at home in winter. I was not able to write to Erica at the moment, nor was I able to telephone her, our last meeting ended in a dispute! This was probably not yet completely forgiven, not yet completely digested - I needed a little more time.

I browsed a little in a bookstore, where I bought a biography about the Indian freedom fighter and philosopher Sri Aurobindo and as well a book about Ayurvedic medicine. I had lunch in a small, quiet garden-restaurant. I ordered a chicken curry, and after a long time I granted myself a bottle of *Kingfisher* beer. The restaurant was quite well occupied with Western tourists. While waiting for my meal, I had time to listen to their conversations - it was another world. The conversations revolved mainly around where they had already been, and where they were going next, and how much they had been cheated at bargaining. At the table behind me an Italian couple argued in a muffled, pressed voice. Obviously, he didn't like the food...I understand some Italian and snapped up when she, a slightly chubby, resolute woman, hissed loudly at him: "Why don't you go home to your *mama*, eat your spaghetti and lasagna there!"

I am not gloating, I was aware of how unpleasant such a partner quarrel is...a quiet laugh, however, I could not hide. I had already noticed several times that these spoiled Italian *Granny's* and *Mama's* boys had a hard time with Indian food.

As soon as my meal was served, Caterina entered the restaurant. She looked around for an empty seat, recognized me and sat down at the same table. Caterina wore a blue headscarf today with gold-colored embroidery, in which she reminded me even more of Nefertiti...Caterina had already eaten, she just wanted to drink a lassi and rest a little while.

"Have you had enough of Swami's lime water?" she joked, pointing to my beer.

"Nothing against Swami's lime water, but a beer now and then is not to be scoffed at. I drank the last one three weeks ago, I hardly remembered what it tasted like."

Of course, I told Caterina about this sad funeral I had experienced in the morning.

Caterina reacted in a shocked but calm manner.

She'd obviously had some experience in this country...

"What do you think of the Swami?" Caterina wanted to know, "How did you meet him?"

I told her under what kind of circumstances I had met him, that I was quite scared and that I had been under the tree seven years ago.

Caterina in turn told how she had met the Swami:

"I have had a similar experience as you, I as well was quite frightened when I first met the Swami...I lived in your area for a while, often I went for a swim at this part of the beach because the coast is not that steep. I always used the tree as cloth changing room One morning I came to the tree, took off my clothes, slipped into my swimsuit and went swimming. Back under the tree I took off my wet swimsuit and dried myself. When I loosened my hair band - at that time I wore long hair - a voice suddenly said; "What a beautiful morning view, beautiful sister – Today Shiva means it especially well with me!"

I couldn't believe my eyes - there this old Swami cracker sits happily on a slightly raised branch, palms joined together for an Indian greeting. "Good Morning beautiful sister", he continued, "I didn't want to scare you!"

Yes sure, I was quite scared, I had never met anyone under the tree before, I had become quite carefree, I noticed traces in the sand in the morning, but I assumed that maybe the fishermen's children had been playing under the tree.

"Beautiful sister, I won't hurt you, I'm an old man", he reassured me, "it is not my fault that you use my new apartment as a cloth changing room, I've been living here since yesterday!"

We both had to laugh, the ice was broken – "I am not a prude, just a little scared - it is probably one of his peculiarities to register in the life of the others with a fright. I love the Swami very much, he's a genius in his own way. His art of living, his way of thinking, how he analyses things, takes them apart and puts them back together again is brilliant!"

"I also like the Swami very much! It is a privilege to live with him under this tree. I'm learning a lot from him. I didn't know until now that one can think like that, that one can see things that way, that one can interpret connections that way. I feel like at home under this tree with the Swami, it is the most beautiful place I have ever lived in and the Swami is the wisest person I have ever met. But I never have the feeling that he is my guru, shaman or Swami, we are more like good friends and buddies, it is often funny and chummy. A feeling tells me that I am only at the beginning with the Swami, that there is still a lot to come..."

"I think your feeling, Eno, is not deceiving you. Whoever knows the Swami goes through a school without him noticing!"

"By the way, Caterina, I'm going to see the Swami today by the Shiva Temple at the full moon festival. Would you like to come with me?"

"Thanks for the invitation, Eno, unfortunately I don't have time today, I have a few things to do, I also have to go to an injured sick person, to Dave, a friend who broke his leg."

"He must have come to India to skiing", I joked.

"No, he walked into a manhole on the street with no lid. But in reality, he rushed and walked through life too quickly, looking neither left nor right. Now he is forced to walk slowly with two crutches - those who do not listen to the inner voice will sooner or later feel it outside. Dave has literally been racing through his life. On the street he walked three times faster than anybody else. I met Dave while trekking in Nepal, we were in a group of six. Dave has rushed over the mountains like possessed...without really looking, without rest and quiet, unable to really enjoy - now he has the chance to learn exactly that. - Every physical suffering is the indirect or direct cause of mental suffering! - Another example, Eno, a few years ago I was the singer of a London pop band. Our drummer wanted to quit, he didn't like it anymore, wanted to do something else. Fearing not to disappoint anyone, not to endanger the band, he did not dare to take this step. So, he lived in a constant conflict for months... Should I or should I not? Finally, he was redeemed - he broke his wrist joint while skating. Ultimately, everyone looks for his accident, his illness himself, the subconscious is looking for it - every illness, every accident, results in the end from a psychological conflict. This psychological conflict is the cause of a defect, an illness, an accident. When the spiritual cause has been found, the recovery, the healing also progresses.

Those who are able to recognize and interpret the psychological conflict early on and make the right decision will have fewer accidents and will be ill less often."

"Why must man suffer at all, Caterina?"

"That man may learn from his illness in suffering. Often illness and suffering are the things that make people understand. Buddha says: *Life is suffering*. I think he has got the point."

After the second lassi Caterina said goodbye. I ordered a coffee, which I sipped slowly, ruminating about suffering and illness.

I went to the bus station, where there was a busy, industrious chaos. The buses drove at walking pace, honking, leaving black diesel clouds behind them, through the luggage dragging, shouting crowds. Because all bus schedules and timetables were written in Tamil script, it took me quite a while to find the right bus. This one had already started the engine. From the radio loudspeakers boomed at full volume, raging, deafening Bollywood sound. I managed to get one of the last free seats in the back of the bus, which shortly afterwards started to move, honking non-stop and slowly making its way through the crowd. Trapped between two fat Indians, I sat on a bench for three. Fortunately, the person sitting at the window got out after half an hour, so that I could slide down. The rocking ride over hundreds of potholes, some of which were pot tubs, took about two hours. Rather shaken and half seasick I finally reached Tiruvannamali, at the foot of Mt. Arunachala The Shiva Temple could not be overlooked, from far away one could see four pyramid-shaped towers, thirty yards high, one in each cardinal direction, the entrance gates to the inner temple place.

In the huge temple complex the full moon festival was already in full swing...drums, rattles, timpani and tablas, pipes and horns mixed into an incredible sound. Flying merchants offered all kinds of food, snacks, sweets, toys and flower garlands...Beggars, Monks, Swamis, Sadhus and a few thousand pilgrims from all over India - a fragrance of a hundred kinds of incense, spices, and perfumes hovered over everything. I sat down on a wall ledge, bought a *chai* from a flying trader, watched the colorful insane madness for a while - it was pulsating, vibrating Indian ecstasy pure!

Then I set off, letting the stream of pilgrims drive me towards the south portal - by the left tower, he had said...and then I saw him...A few steps to the left of it, in front of a big column, my Swami sat in *lotus* seat on a raffia mat, in front of him a begging bowl. It was highly unusual to see him, dressed in only one thong, in this environment, in this turmoil. From some distance I watched him for a moment, it became clear to me how close he was to me, how much I had taken him into my heart.
"Hey, hello, old Swami", I greeted him, "may I join you?"

"Hello, Eno, there you are! Don't be modest if you don't mind sitting next to a beggar. It's best if you sit on my left side.

"It is an honor to sit next to you Swami, for me you are anything but a beggar, for me it is a privilege to know you. By the way, Caterina sends her regards; we met at *Les Amis*. I also called my parents in Switzerland. There is nearly laying a five inches of snow, the mercury shows minus five degrees - you would look quite old with your string thong!"

"Brrr"...shuddered the Swami, "just thinking about it, gives me the creeps."

Of course, I also told the Swami what had happened in the morning in front of our door on the beach.

"Eno, I have lived in India for thirty years, I have experienced things here and seen things, positive and negative, for which there are no words or imagination. India is an infinite cosmos in itself. I ask myself every day how this cosmos works. There are moments when I think I've broken the code. In the next moment I realize that I have understood nothing at all. Maybe that's why I've been here for thirty years - because I'm trying to crack the Indian code!

The begging bowl was well filled, the Swami thanked the respective donor by placing the palms of his hands together at chest level and saying "Shiva blesses you."

There were also pilgrims who donated a little bit more, asked the Swami for an advice, request for a special blessing. Among all the Sadhus, Gurus, Swamis and Mendicants the Swami was a kind of star - the Indians had never seen a white Swami from the west! His advice, his blessing seemed to be much desirable and popular. Sometimes a whole bunch of people stood around us. When it became too much for the Swami, he evicted away the whole gang like a swarm of flies with a wave of his hand.

A very fat, chubby-cheeked man, who wore a giant ring on each finger, well dressed for the occasion, crouched down with us, placed a 20 Rupee note in the begging bowl.

"Holy Yogi, *namaste*! I have a question - what does my future look like, how will my business work?"

The Swami looked, as only he could, long and deep into the eyes of the man.

"List for me all you have eaten today, there lies a part of the truth about your future", he asked him.

The man faithfully listed everything he had eaten for morning, lunch, dinner and in between. It seemed as if he didn't want to stop enumerating. A huge quantity gathered where I would probably eat for two or three days...!

"I thought so, I suspected so", said the Swami seriously. "I can assure you of one thing for sure, if you continue to eat so much, stuff everything inside you, your future looks like...you will soon have none! Your heart is over fatted, your blood pressure is way too high. You'll die early - of a heart attack, then you won't have to worry about business. I give you a good advice, eat two thirds less, do half an hour of Yoga every day, then you will become more flexible and agile, not only physically, but also in business - Shiva bless you!"

"Thank you, holy Yogi, I will follow your advice - may you live long", the fat man replied, he rose groaning and went away.

I was speechless - that was pretty direct, not very diplomatic...

Before I could say anything, a disturbed, pregnant, slightly limping woman came to us with a swollen eye. She put five Rupees in the bowl.

"Holy Swami, I ask you for a blessing for my unborn child - may it be born healthy", she said.

"You, beautiful daughter of Parvati", said the Swami, "before I bless your child and you, I would like to see your husband first. Where is he?"

"He's waiting back there by the sugarcane stand", the woman replied somewhat uncertainly.

"Get him!" the Swami commanded.

The woman went to her husband. From a distance it looked, as if he didn't really want to come along...after all they came in twos.

"Look into my eyes", the Swami told the man. "Why does your wife limp? Where did the swollen eye come from?" he asked curtly.

"My wife stumbled unhappily two days ago, fell down the stairs and injured herself", her husband replied.

"Is it true?" the Swami asked the woman. She lowered her eyes embarrassed, gave no answer..."Since your wife does not answer, I assume that you are lying, that you told me the untruth", the Swami said sharply. "I know the real story, listen carefully! You hit your wife and, deliberately pushed her down the stairs...am I right?"

Both held their gaze lowered, saying nothing...you could clearly see that they felt extremely uncomfortable.

"You wanted your wife to lose your child because she's an unwanted daughter. You had made an ultrasound test - the child in your wife's womb is a baby girl, isn't it?! You hurt your beautiful wife, you put your unborn sweet daughter in grave danger - you are a son of a bitch, a murderer!"

The man looked absolutely miserable, the woman was shivering slightly.

"If the fruit in your wife's womb was a son", the Swami continued, "you would both be carrying them on your hands - but because it is an unwanted daughter, both of them have to pay for it - you have loaded yourself with a damn bad, fucking karma! - You can only compensate for this to some extent by showing remorse, loving and treating your wife and daughter well in the future. A woman is worth as much as a man, a daughter is worth as much as a son! Do you understand me? If I hear that you do not treat your wife and daughter well, I will personally slay you like a mangy dog. - I bless your wife and your sweet little daughter! By all the gods, may she be born healthy! Before I can bless you, come back here in a year and show me your heart - and now go!"

I felt really queasy, the whole scene was really intense...I had never experienced the Swami so fiery and hard. His gestures, his gaze, his facial expressions, the haunting, convincing voice - he embodied absolute authority! For a moment I was a little bit afraid for him...the guy from before seemed to be quite strong, he surely could have knocked the Swami out with one punch! But what the Swami said - especially the way he said it - was so direct, disarming and true that you could only swallow empty.

"Wow, Swami...that was strong tobacco! Don't you think that was a little bit too much of a good thing? The guy had some serious muscles...for a moment I thought he will smack you in the face."

"No, what are you thinking? That wasn't too much of a good thing – I'm not afraid of such creatures. Besides, he couldn't afford to hit an old, holy Swami. It would cause a great attract attention here, a tremendous tumult. No, no, my friend, that wasn't too much of a good thing - do you think I can say to this dog;

"Dear *Babu*, never do something like that again! Where would I go? He'll never forget my lesson. He's got it in the bone marrow! I only see the guy once in my life time, for a few minutes - I can't do a lot of therapy, I have to be really tough, give him hell fire, other-wise I don't stand a chance!"

Usually the Swami was friendly and kind. In his speeches and teachings there was always a humorous, sarcastic undertone - that was just his way! People seemed to like it. He gave everyone what he needed. With unerring accuracy, he picked out those elements which needed a wooden hammer.

We were also photographed from time to time, the Swami always greeted in Indian style, looked well-behaved or grim, it all depended on the person taking the picture. A rich Indian man who thought he was something very special - a really arrogant asshole with dark sunglasses even wanted to place himself between the Swami and me for the photo. The Swami put on his super look and said, "If you want me to move my ass for you, my friend, it will cost you a hundred Rupees."

Without making a face, the guy took a big pack of banknotes from his breast pocket, gave the Swami a hundred. He moved one yard to the side, whereupon this guy sat down in our midst. His wife took pictures of the three of us - I was quite embarrassed.

"Where do you come from?" he asked.

"For you, my friend, each question costs a hundred Rupees."

Once again, this guy pulled out a hundred bucks without making a face.

"I am originally from Germany", the Swami replied irritable, "do you want to know something else?"

The guy denied it, stood up, said, "Thank you", and took his wife for a stroll...

We looked at each other diagonally for a moment, shook our heads and moved together again – unbelievable! - There are arrogant people in every country and culture, but an arrogant Indian is not to be overbid!"

In quieter moments, the Swami emptied the begging bowl, separated the paper money from the coins, put both in his bag.

Meanwhile it was dawning. Colorful light bulbs, torches, candles and small lamps replaced the daylight. From inside the temple now sounded timpani and drums.

"Hey Swami, I think I'm going to sightseeing for a bit, try to get into the temple - I want to see what's going on there."

To the right of the temple entrance there was a huge portal where every visitor had to take off and deposit his shoes. On the left side of the portal the wealthy Indians deposited their expensive shoes for a fee. The right side, where no fee was charged, was reserved for the plastic slippers of the poorer people. There were a few thousand plastic slippers there. Eighty percent of them were in blue, like mine - how did everyone find his slippers again? I tried to remember mine by a small torn spot on the left strap.

Barefoot I went now to the main entrance, where I bought a half coconut shell filled with flowers for twenty Rupees as entrance fee from a temple student.

I lined up in the queue of people, which slowly moved temple inwards. From another temple disciple I got a white point dotted on my forehead, another one lit a paraffin cube, which he placed burning in my coconut shell half. Slowly our queue moved forward, past frescoes, columns and shrines towards the temple center, where a three yard's high golden Shiva statue was enthroned in lotus position on a stone pedestal, holding a bowl of fire in its lap. The *Om* chanting and drums sounded louder and louder, more and more ecstatic, created an all-pervading vibration, I too sang *Om* with full fervor. The golden Shiva statue shone, glowing in the light of a thousand paraffin cubes and candles placed on and around the pedestal. I also placed the flowers with the burning paraffin cube at Shiva's feet, made the Indian greeting sign and moved away towards the exit. Finally, I threw my empty coconut shell half, imitating the Indians, against a stone *Shivalingam*, where it broke into several pieces - supposed to bring good luck. The *Puja* ceremony was over - when I think back to my stiff Cristian confirmation...

Indeed, I found my plastic slippers again! Strolling a little more through the festival grounds, I stopped here and there, watching this and that. On a staircase I saw an old Indian *Sadhu* sitting, whose beard was a single two yards long dreadlock, twice wrapped around his body. The old man beckoned me to him.

"Hello, traveler from the West, *namaste*!", he said. "I am the best palm reader all over India - would you like to have a little taste? I'll tell you how many brothers and sisters you have."

-If you find that out, I thought - then you're not bad, because I'm an only child."

I sat down on the stairs next to the old sadhu and held out my right hand to him. Gently he took my hand and put it in his own. He touched it deeply, caressed it lovingly, studied it carefully.

"You are the only son of your parents", he said after a while, "you have no brothers or sisters."

"Well done, not bad, old Swami, I am surprised! You do know your art. I actually do not have any brothers or sisters."

"You see, young friend, I did not promise too much. For a small donation I'll be very grateful, you won't regret it."

"Okay, Baba, you convinced me. Here's a hundred Rupees - show me what else you got on!"

"Young master, you are very generous - Shiva be with you! I'll do my best!"

Once again, the old man studied my hand thoroughly.

"Young friend," he continued, "you are born under a rare star. You are already many incarnations old, have been in this world many times! Your path of life, your destiny, will not be easy, but it will be full of knowledge and consciousness - in old age you will be a wise man. Your vocation is an extraordinary one!

At the moment you are in an intense process of transformation, in a fateful phase of your life, which is decisive for your vocation. But success only comes in the last third of your life. The love of your life is waiting for you. But you will only recognize it when you have found your vocation.

You have a very close relationship with your mother and a very distant relationship with your father. Isn't it?"

"It's like this, old Swami!"

The old man let go of my hand and blessed me by stroking the end of his dreadlock beard over my head I had to laugh...

"Well, how was it?", the Swami asked when I was back again with him.

"Awesome, man, cool party! Just a moment ago I met a palm reader, one with a two yards long dreadlock beard. He read my palm. Among other things, he found out that I am an only child - that impressed me quite a lot!"

"Really? I'm glad you met him, Eno. There is only one with such a beard - Swami Mahananda Rishi, a wise man, one of the best palm readers in India."

"The temple ceremony was very beautiful, Swami. Christians would probably call this *idolatry*, like Moses and the golden calf - but Shiva is not a calf! Shiva is the God of destruction and renewal in one - the destruction of the old that gives way to the new! I think that Shiva has just as much a right to exist as a Buddha statue or a figure of the Savior on the cross."

"I agree with you, Eno, Shiva is the first origin Shaman, he is much older than Hinduism, he already existed when there were no religions. He was integrated into Hinduism much later - you couldn't just take away people's Shiva! Inquisition has been less squeamish, our Druids and Shamans have been killed, their *pagan* symbols have been destroyed - with the result, that today we do not allow magic, ecstasy and visions - instead we create artificial television that stunts and dulls our minds.

Jesus, by the way, was a wise and enlightened man", continued the Swami, "one who sought and assembled the mirror of truth. Did you know, Eno, Jesus lived in India for many years, in his biography, there is a piece, a part missing, where we don't know exactly where he was and what he did. The Bible says he returned to his Father in heaven for a few years to study. This is of course nonsense! Not even Jesus can do that, in the end he too was only a man of flesh and blood, albeit an enlightened one. Jesus pilgrimaged the ancient Silk-Road from Judea to India. He probably lived as a Monk in a Krishna temple and was enlightened there - the name Christ is probably derived from Krishna. After a few years he returned home and preached his teaching, what he had learned. He was the first guru in the West, and at the same time the most successful! - Guru means "spiritual master".

And now, Eno, hold on! We sit in a time machine and fly back to the year 33 AD, to Mount Golgotha... The wise, enlightened Guru Jesus, who proclaims the doctrine of love, the law of Karma, is then crucified by the Romans. The Jewish pharisees, who saw their power, their polarizing, *eternal hell or heaven* faith in danger, denounced him to the Romans, the occupiers in Judea, and arrested him on Mount Golgotha by Roman soldiers and then he got crucified.

Today the cross is used as a Christian symbol throughout the Christian world...but Jesus had nothing to do with the cross at all. Jesus used two fishes as a symbol. The Christian symbol represented two fishes for five hundred years. The original Christians still use this symbol today. The Catholics who split off from the original Christians, introduced the cross as a Christian symbol – Imagine Eno, if they had hanged Jesus, we would probably have a gallows as a symbol today...the Catholics distorted, censored and manipulated the original teachings of Christ completely. They took over the dual heaven and hell thinking from the Jews and used the crucified-one as a symbol of admonition - do not seek the mirror of truth yourself - otherwise you will end up like Jesus! Do not eat from the tree of knowledge, or you will be expelled from paradise!

Bullshit - what the fuck is wrong with knowledge?!

I can tell you, Eno, it was just the opposite of what it says in the Bible. The "Great Spirit" has namely said: "Eat of the tree of knowledge, and you will enter paradise Do not be afraid of the serpent. Eve's apple was not just a simple fruit apple from some apple tree. Eve's apple stands for the psychoactive shamanic plants that give us knowledge and insight and liberty, with whose help we can look into paradise!

The cross, Eno, is one of the most destructive and bloody symbols of all...The blood of millions of people is on the cross - even the blood of the Savior! The cross has the same shape as the sword, the sword the same shape as the cross.

Imagine that on the crusades, the priests walked in front with the cross in their hands, and behind them the crusaders slaughtered everything short and small with the sword, the same symbol. In contrast to the cross, the energy flow of a circle appears harmonious, round and infinite. The energy flow of a cross is angular and edgy, it collides in the middle at the cross point, there is a jam, a knot, the flow of cosmic energy is disturbed, similar to a road junction. At a roundabout everything is always in flow.

When all the crosses have disappeared from the churches and been replaced by circles, when all the moon sickles in the mosques have been exchanged for a full moon, things will improve on earth. If we worship the circle and the ball, instead of the cross and the sickle, a transformation has taken place within us - we have become truly aware of the cycle, the incarnations and eternity."

"Wow, Swami! The way you compose all this together is just brilliant!"

"That, Eno, is the art of seeking the shards of the mirror and putting the mirror of truth back together properly."

During the last ten minutes while Swami was talking to me, not a single pilgrim had come to us, the Indians seemed to sense that I was just getting a special lesson.

A group of twenty tourists from Japan besieged and took pictures of us. We both raised our hands to the Indian greeting, the Swami grinned mischievously, I smiled cool. The cameras were buzzing and clicking, the flashes flickering.

I thought...Let the Japs take their pictures...

The Swami held up the begging bowl and shouted: "Honda, Suzuki, Kawasaki, Yamaha! You people from the land of the rising sun, I love your great inventions and your busy beekeeping."

The Japanese grinned politely, took more photos, eagerly donated Rupees.

"Whel do you come flom?", they wanted to know. When the Swami said: "Flom Gelmani', everyone went "Oh' and "Ah' in amazement, their mouths almost didn't close anymore.

A Western tourist, one of these photographer freaks, took several pictures of the Swami and donated just two Rupees afterwards!

"You, miserly photo maniac!" the Swami shouted loudly, some Indians looked in amazement. "Lumpy two Rupees for a famous Swami! – Shame on you! I hope you got the film upside down, you scrooge! You're one of those photo junkies, always looking for the next shot. I hope they soon steal your shit camera!" The Swami shouted with flailing arms, the guy looked that he could disappear...

But the Swami had another side as well: An ancient, wrinkled woman with infinitely sad eyes, who probably didn't have very long to live, grinding poor, walking hunched on a stick, came along dragging. She wanted to crouch down to us, but the Swami stood up, hugged the old mother, stroking her grey hair gently for a while. A big tear was rolling out of one of her sad eyes.

I was touched - this scene needed no words...

In the meanwhile, it had become around eleven o'clock at night. I was faced with the choice of going through the night or taking the first early morning bus back together with the Swami, or soon going home alone on the last night bus. It had been a long and eventful day. I longed for sleep, for the tranquility of our tree. So, I decided to set off slowly. The Swami gave me all his coins, which weighed at least a half of a pound.

"This way I don't have to carry so much weight tomorrow, I'm sure there'll be a lot more coming together."

With some effort and struggle I caught one of the last seats in an old, rusty, windowless diesel bus, which howled full speed through the night. The saris, cloths, blankets and *lungis* fluttered in the wind of the passage. While changing gears, the whole bus vibrated, rumbled, groaned and moaned. My sleeping neighbor nestled his head against my shoulder. With every pothole he slipped a little more towards me. My polite request for consideration didn't help much, he fell asleep quick again and confound my shoulder with his resting pillow once again. After a while I had enough, felt myself uncomfortable, got tired of it... at the next big pothole I helped along a bit, gave the guy with the shoulder half a chin hook - from then on I had my peace. Although, this affectionate guy now snuggled up to the other neighbor who was sitting at the window seat - this mixture of ruthless implicitness and ignorance is something you often encounter in India. I was glad when the bus finally arrived in Pondicherry, at the bus station. For the remaining five miles to our village I tucked a motor rickshaw.

It was about two o'clock at night, the village was dark, deserted. The shops and food stalls were all closed and boarded up, only a few dogs were roaming around. Such a stray, hungry, dog pack was not without danger. Beaten and kicked during the day, they could become very dangerous to a single person at night.

Undisturbed, I reached the tree where I found everything untouched - how nice to be home again! I hided the coins in the Sand, brushed my teeth, then rolled myself into my blanket. It was the first time I slept alone under the tree. I was here for about five weeks now - what had I not experienced in this time! At the moment nothing pulled me away from here, I felt safe and at home, maybe more than ever before somewhere else. Protected by the tree, watched over by the cobra, I fell asleep with the sound of the waves.

The next morning, after a swim in the sea, followed by the obligatory freshwater shower, I went to Amukaram to get a huge portion of *Idlis* and coffee. Peacefully eating and sipping coffee I enjoyed the morning silent under our tree. I was in a great mood. I felt balanced, cheerful and elated, connected to everything in a beautiful way, as a part of the whole.

Later in the morning the Swami returned from the full moon festival. Considering that he had been through the whole night, had two hours of bumpy bus ride behind him and counted eighty-two winters, he seemed surprisingly fresh and lively.

"How glad I am to be back home", he moaned, "this peace, the sight of the sea – I have enough of the full moon festival for a month."

We sat together for a while, then the Swami went to sleep well deservedly. I was browsing a little more in the two books I had bought the day before.

Afterwards I washed some clothes by the draw well. Just when I was finished, Shanti showed up with a full laundry basket. I melted at the sight of her as always - she looked absolutely sweet and adorable!

"Hello, Miss, how are you today?" I greeted.

"Very good, thank you", she replied.

I inquired about the condition of her family, asked her a few general things. She understood and spoke better English than I had thought.

"You speak English very well", I noticed, "better than most men from the village."

She told that she had attended school for four years and had learned a little English there.

"It was nice to see you and talk to you - I wish you a nice day, goodbye, see you..."

"Thank you, you are very nice", she replied - I felt like I was in seventh heaven...this short conversation, this touch of flirt, with this beautiful woman from another culture so foreign to me was more mysterious and enchanting than any hot flirt or dating in a Western bar or discotheque.

I simply hung my wet laundry on the outside of the tree on the branches to dry. In the Indian sun these light cotton clothes dried in one hour.

The Swami was still sleeping, I went to Amukaram's food stall where I enjoyed an Indian *Thali*. Amukaram had a toothache today, so he looked a bit worn out and was a little less in good spirits. He wanted the tooth pulled out the next day. I promised to bring him a painkiller for the night.

Back at the tree, the Swami had gotten up in the meantime. He was sorting and counting his income from the temple festival. He had taken 2500 Rupees. A large part of the money consisted of one, two and five Rupee bank notes, most of them were quite faulty and tattered. Many of the pilgrims donated their old, tattered bank notes, which they could not get rid of anywhere. In India there are a lot of totally rotten banknotes in circulation, especially the small notes are often tattered and worn out. You always have to be careful not to receive them, because it is very difficult to get rid of them. Exchanging them for *new ones* on a bank is not so easy, a huge procedure, that can take half a day. And often the new notes do not look much better than the old ones.

The work now consisted of patching up these old notes with transparent Scotch tape. Some were literally held together only by their own dirt. Because the Swami had no ID, he could not go to any bank anyway So he collected the worst specimens and occasionally exchanged them in the slum for a ten percent commission.

In the evening after dinner we sat together in the light of the kerosene lamp and chatted a bit.

"What exactly is the meaning of life? Why and what for are we all here?", I asked the Swami.

"The purpose of life is to gain knowledge and awareness and love, that is why we are or would be here."

"How to attain consciousness, knowledge and love Swami?"

"By seeking the shards of the broken mirror of truth and putting them back together again correctly - with every shard you found, your knowledge, love and your consciousness expands. You see more and more clearly. Unfortunately, only very few people take care of their consciousness, most of them let it really shrink and atrophy away, that is why they are not wise but senile in old age. Very few people ask about the real meaning of life, most people deal with all kinds of nonsense. Seeking the meaning of life is not simply the job of philosophers - it is the meaning of all of us, the task of all of us."

"Consciousness, Swami, is a great concept, what exactly does it contain, how can one define consciousness?"

"The consciousness contains: Love, tolerance, ethics and respect, the knowledge of the why and wherefore of birth, life and death, the knowledge of the cycle of incarnations. A conscious person has the ability to look behind the scenes, below the surface of things. He has the ability to communicate with the Great Spirit and the genetic information of his own DNA.

"How do I attain consciousness and knowledge, Swami, what I have to do specifically for this?"

"There are shamanic and yoga techniques that expand consciousness. There are also a few good books that can help. In the case of books, however, there is a danger that knowledge will remain only theoretical and intellectual. Conscious vision, conscious experience is missing. It's like when I go to car driving school, and I only make the theoretically driving test. I will then know about the traffic rules, but I will never have the feeling, the experience of driving a car. Everything requires a technique, a vehicle. In order to expand the consciousness, to reach the so-called enlightenment, yoga techniques or shamanic vehicles are needed."

"I can imagine of something under yoga techniques. What exactly do you mean by shamanic vehicles, Swami?"

Shaman vehicles are usually psychoactive plants or mushrooms, with the help of them we are allowed to look into paradise, there we get an insight how things really are. The universal truth."

The next morning the Swami left early, taking advantage of the morning chill, to go into town to visit an old friend. Because I felt a bit lazy and weak, I preferred to stay at home.

"It may be late at night by the time I get back", he said as he left.

I dozed a little while more, bathed in the sea, watched a pair of buzzards which had moved to our neighboring palm tree, to build a nest there. Apparently, the male bird, protested and rejected to my sitting in front of our tree. The bird attacked me several times by flying towards me in a nosedive with angled wings. Shortly above me it opened its wings and flew half a foot above my head, once its claws almost touched my forehead. The wing span was about four feet. For moments our eyes met, we were eye to eye - What a magnificent bird!

Between our tree and the grove there was a flat, sandy area about fifty by fifty yards in size, with an old fireplace in the middle. Munching fruit salad and sipping coffee, I watched through the leaves a man pushing a bicycle, heavily loaded with dry wood, to the fireplace, the bicycle was hardly visible under all the wood. After he had unloaded the wood and piled it next to the fireplace, he disappeared

I wondered what he was up to...after a while the man returned heavily loaden, unloaded the wood and disappeared again. The scenario was repeated a total of three times. In the end there was an amount of three cubic yard of thick, good wood together. The man now lifted the fireplace a little bit with a hoe, covered the ground with a layer of medium-thick logs, and placed a layer of straw on top. I had seen the fireplace many times before, it was washed out by the monsoon, seemed to be quite unused. A few times I had burnt some rubbish there. I decided to ask the man what the occasion for such a big fire was. I went to see him. We greeted each other politely and respectfully in the Indian way. Unfortunately, he did not speak a word of English. I couldn't quite make out his language, his gestures. He repeatedly imitated the sign for sleep by holding a hand to the side of his head and closing his eyes...at bedtime in the night some celebration, some occasion had to take place, I interpreted. Somehow the guy seemed a little creepy and aloof. Around his lean, angular head with a hooked nose, he had pirate-like wrapped a white cloth deep into his forehead, under which a pair of deep, piercing, dark eyes peered out. Around his waist he wore a blue *lungi* with a dagger in it. The upper body was undressed. The man's working movements were precise and exact - no movement too much, no movement too little, every log had exactly its place. When the work was done, he left. I could tell from his gestures that he would come back in the evening.

In the late afternoon - I was just dozing a little - I was suddenly awakened by human voices, chanting and drumming. I peeked through the leaves. At some distance I saw about two dozen men approaching the fireplace in a kind of procession. First in front of all, four men carried a bamboo rack with a flower-decorated bamboo frame. When they arrived at the fireplace, they put the rack on the floor. On closer inspection I could make out a long, white bale of fabric on the rack between all the flowers...Slowly I understood - the rack was a bier with a flowered bamboo structure. On the bier laid a dead person wrapped in a white cloth. This dead person should be cremated here.

Now I also saw the man who had brought all the wood in the morning. He again was busy with the fireplace, some men helped him. I assumed he was the undertaker, the cremator. The mourners, all of them men, stood or sat around in small groups discussing. I felt quite disturbed and uncomfortable! Not even thirty steps away from my peaceful tree home, a community of two dozen people moved around, to burn their dead - why did the Swami leave me alone exactly today? How should I act in the face of this situation? Should I show myself to the people or was it more appropriate to stay under the tree? A group of mourners sat very close to the tree in the shade. The danger was great that they would discover me. I had no idea how they would react. I tried to imagine how a half-naked Indian with a tourist visa would live in Switzerland on a cemetery under a tree - unimaginable!

The corpse was now placed in the prepared hollow by four men and covered in several layers with thick logs of wood - the cremation preparations now seemed to be completed.

Gesturing, the cremator spoke to a group of men, including a policeman, constantly pointing at my tree. All men now looked at my tree in amazement.

Oh dear, I hope there's no trouble now!

The cremator now broke away from the group and slowly walked to my tree. I took a deep breath, tried to arrange my tangled hair a little bit with my hands, tried to appear somewhat present.

Already the branches were parting at the tree entrance... The cremator stood in front of me, raised his hands for an Indian greeting, I did the same, a little perplexed. He made inviting gestures that I should come with him. Because I was only wearing shorts, I quickly slipped on a shirt. With slightly strange feelings I finally followed him to the cremation site. The mourners were quite astonished when they saw their cremator emerging out of the tree together with a half-naked white guy. The men, however, did not seem to be discontented, indignant or otherwise against me in any way. I greeted all the present men collectively by placing the palms of my hands together and closing my eyes for a moment as a sign of my sympathy and condolence.

At a proper distance from the stake, I sat down on the ground near a group of men. One of the men offered me a cigarette, invited me to sit with them. I took the offer and squatted in the round. Almost all men now lit cigarettes or *bidis*. We sat together, puffing comfortably - I was taken in by them.

The curiosity, the astonishment about my presence quickly subsided, the people devoted themselves to their work again. The man who had invited me to smoke spoke some English, he told me that the dead was an old man from the neighboring village.

The cremator now demanded his attention. He spoke a short prayer and then fell into a monotonous chant, during which the son of the deceased circled the stake three times, sprinkling petrol from a clay pot over the wood. Then he lit a torch with which he lit the pyre.

Slowly the first flames were flickering, the cremation fire was setting itself on fire.

It was a strange feeling, never in my life I had attended a funeral or cremation. And now I was here in India attending a Hindu open-air cremation of a person unknown to me...It was a huge difference to our Western high-tech cremation facilities and stiff funerals - here, the whole scene was almost like a campfire. There was a lack of Western order, discipline and piety. The mourners all sat or stood around discussing in groups. Although I did not understand their language, but I had the impression that they were talking about the problems of life rather than death. Of course, everyone wanted to know where I come from, what I do here, what my name is, what profession I do. Even with the son of the deceased I made small talk. He was visibly proud that a European was paying his father his last respects.

I also had a little chat with the policeman. He was interested in the color of the Swiss police uniforms. He did not ask for my passport, nor did he want to see the tourist visa. I could watch how the son of the deceased haggled with the cremator about the funeral costs, finally they agreed by handshake.

A rickshaw driver, who smelled quite strongly of *Arrak* brandy, started bawling and shouting at people. He wanted me to marry his daughter, again and again he praised her beauty, praised all her qualities, until the cremator rebuked him with loud words.

After an hour, the fire was still burning brightly, the funeral guests set off for the village. Most men said goodbye to me with a handshake or waved goodbye.

Alone with the cremator I stayed on the areal. Meanwhile it had become dark, the short time of twilight was over. The huge fire lit up the whole place. The cremator had brought his dinner in a military galley, he invited me to eat with him. He scooped up my portion on the lid of the galley and handed me two chapatis. So, we sat in silence in the sand and ate. The cremator did not seem to be a man of many words, he still seemed a little eerie to me, radiating an aura of aloofness. I guess it had something to do with his profession. But I could sense that he liked me somehow. The chicken curry his wife had cooked tasted delicious.

After dinner he asked: "Coooffi?" I nodded and said, "Yes!"

The cremator stood up, emptied some water from a plastic canister he had brought with him into a small aluminum pot, placed it on the hot embers at the edge of the fire. The fire had an insane heat, within seconds the water was boiling. Some instant coffee, milk powder and sugar - and the coffee was ready.

Silently we stared into the flames, sipped the coffee, smoked a *bidi*. After the coffee, he rinsed the dishes with the remaining water from the canister and tied the tools and utensils he had brought along on his bicycle. Then he said goodbye, telling me coming back tomorrow.

Since I had assumed that the cremator would look after the fire all night and keep vigil, I was somewhat surprised at the sudden departure. The cremator could not leave me alone with such a huge fire - he had apparently never heard of responsibility before!

It was hard to believe...there I was sitting all alone, as a Westerner, ten thousand miles away from home at an Indian cremation fire. I felt a little lonely and left alone. The whole scene was real and unreal, abstract and concrete at the same time.

The fire did not burn as violently as in the beginning. Because the wind blew all the smoke right to our tree, I didn't feel like going there. So, I sat cross-legged and pondered on the side of the dead man's head in front of the fire. With some macabre feelings I tried to detect the head in the embers, but I couldn't see anything...Who might this dead man have been? What was his story? What would he probably say if he saw me now - a Swiss man watching his fire, he would certainly be amazed, it would probably be a surreal scene for him as well.

I also thought about my own death - how, where and under what kind of circumstances would I die one day? I became aware of the whole transience of each individual. In the end, such a body, which has lived for perhaps eighty years, is simply burned or buried...then such a human life is only history, and if there is no one left to remember the story, the story dies too. So, in the end there is nothing left, except perhaps from those people who go in to history, in one way or another, but they are only few in number. Most people are completely forgotten after a few decades, never to be found in any history book.

For a while I was quite melancholic and thoughtful.

What am I doing here? I asked myself - Why am I sitting here? -My friends were on a party or watching TV at that time... and I was here!

It wasn't my duty! -What had that to do with me anyway? Why was the Swami just away today, when he was usually here? Perhaps he knew that a cremation was imminent, had deliberately made a run from it, perhaps he had made an arrangement with the cremator? Maybe he wanted to test me in this way?

I was about to pack my bundle, go to town with a rickshaw, check into a hotel and forget about the whole thing here, including the Swami!

"Hello, Eno, good evening, did you make a bonfire? -I could go for a grilled sausage and a bottle of beer, couldn't you?" I looked at the Swami diagonally...We both had to laugh - I was glad he was back!

"There's been a lot going on here today, Swami. There's a dead man roasting in that fire. The whole staff just took off, including the undertaker, they just left me alone with this huge fire - something like this can only happen in India! Why didn't you tell me that we live next to a cremation place?"

"I just didn't think about it", he replied, "the last cremation took place about two months ago, that is quite a while ago, I just forgot about it. For me it is quite normal to live here - as normal as it is for you next to a kiosk or a post office. The cremator is a friend of mine. He feels very honored that a white Swami from the West lives on his property. It is also a great privilege for me to be so close to death, so I have the best conditions to study him, to deal with him. He has become my friend and ally. I look forward to death, but

I also look forward to each new day of life - the one does not exclude the other."

"Do you believe in life after death, Swami?"

"As I said before, you can leave the believing to those fools who know nothing about anything!

Of course, there's life after death. Death, like birth, it is only a transition to another form of existence. Consciousness is immortal, it is eternal and always. During the process of death, the consciousness detaches itself from the body. It will in some form take on a new material or subtle body in this world or in another. There is not simply heaven and hell forever and ever - that is polarized, dualistic, Christian-Jewish black and white thinking! There are not just two ways, there are different possibilities, perspectives and options. Our world is not the only world. After death, the interstellar journey continues, into another world or back to this world."

"Are there many such worlds, Swami, and how do they differ?"

"According to my calculations, studies and research, there are twenty-four such worlds. They are divided into twelve material and twelve ethereal worlds. Our earth is the twelfth, last earthly world, then slowly the twelve more subtle worlds begin."

"And which of these worlds, Swami, is the best and most beautiful?"

"The twenty-fourth, of course, the last ethereal world. It is the most beautiful, largest, perfect and sublime world - it is the world of worlds! Whoever has reached there is finally at the destination of the journey. Whoever gets there has finished the game."

"And how do I get there, Swami?"

"By playing and holding to the rules and putting together the mirror of truth. It's a long way up there, to the last world. Only those who have found universal truth and universal love may enter it. - Imagine, full of hate, envy, falsehood, selfishness and greed, we enter the last, most beautiful world of the worlds…It would soon be devastated and destroyed!"

"Why, Swami, do you, me, and all the other inhabitants of this world and the other worlds exist? Why does matter even exist? Why is the universe not simply empty, with no planets, no stars? Why is there consciousness at all? And if the Great Spirit created all this, why did he do it and who created him?"

"You may ask questions, Eno! There are no answers to these very big questions in this world - they belong to another mirror which is not meant for this, our world. On the higher, subtle, spiritual worlds we get clearer answers to these questions.

We people of middle-earth should follow the twenty-four rules of the game, respect and honor the Great Spirit, search the glass splitters and assemble our mirror together.

We should be aware that there are other worlds besides our world, that our world is not the highest, most intelligent and most conscious - on the contrary, we should be aware that our world is primitive and backward!"

In silence the Swami and I sat in front of the fire. His words echoed in my ears, and the longer I stared into the embers, the clearer it became, that he was right. Somehow - there had to be other worlds. Our world is certainly not the only one - impossible! This would contradict all physical and mathematical laws!

It was after midnight by now. The cremation fire had turned into a large, red-white glowing pile of coal. I guess the dead man was completely burned.

"Well, Swami, I guess that's it, end of the show, I'm tired and burnt out. I'm going to hit the hay."

"Hey, Eno, old dude, don't give up so quickly. The show's not over yet. We're taking a night off!"

The Swami rose, went under the tree...

With the trident in his hand he came back again. He stuck it into the ground, with the tip of the shaft down. Afterwards the Swami stuffed a *Ganja-Shilom* which we smoked in honor of Shiva - I was suddenly not tired anymore, felt super good.

Now the Swami with the trident began to rake out the pile of embers to form a carpet of about two square meters, to that he was chanting - *Om Shiva Om*. Then he put the trident, one step in front of the embers on the ground.

He came to me, took me by the hand and led me, still chanting *Om*, around the embers three times. In front of the trident we stopped. He indicated to me, to join in his *Om* chanting...beautifully our two *Oms* sounded through the night.

Slowly the Swami faded away, became quieter, I continued chanting alone. He raised his palms to the Indian greeting, bowed before the fire and said: "Holy Shiva, guardian of the fire. God of destruction and renewal, with humility, with respect and esteem I enter the holy fire - *Om Shiva Om*."

Then the Swami jumped over the trident, right into the middle of the red and white glowing carpet of embers – It took my breath away! - I would not have expected that...this insane Swami indeed jumped barefoot into the glittering embers - like another one into the swimming pool. Then he began to dance on this carpet of embers...I took a step back - I had never seen anything like it! - An eighty-two years old man dancing on fire...Even Michael Jackson would have been astonished.

The sparks were flying, the Swami was dancing...For sequences he looked like a teenager, then again, he looked like a hundred years old Indian or Shaman, who turned into Shiva and the next moment and finally became the cunning Rumpelstiltskin. He seemed ageless, infinite and eternal. I saw in him old past lives, sufferings, privations and pains, saw highest happiness, ecstasy, infinite love and wealth. I saw that this Swami was a very special person, a chosen one. I thanked the gods for leading me to him.

After a minute the Swami finished his dance, stepped out of the embers, back on the sandy ground. He put his palms together, thanked Shiva once again, the "Great Spirit", and also the soul of the deceased.

Then the Swami came to me, put his arm around my shoulder and led me to the trident, in front of the fire.

"Eno", he said, "fear is life's greatest enemy. It is the fear that does not let us rise above ourselves - the lack of courage! Fear hinders us, out of fear we do not dare, out of fear we do not risk. Cowardice is the sister of fear. Out of sheer fear and cowardice, we really forget to live and how to really die.

Lord Shiva, guardian of the fire, give my young friend the strength and courage to dance on your holy fire. Burn his fear, doubt and cowardice. Harden and purify him with your holy fire - *Om Shiva Om*!"

The Swami let go off my shoulder, took a few steps away, started to sing the *Om* singing again.

I stood alone in front of the fire...The heat of the orange-red, yellow-white carpet of embers was mercilessly beating against me...In there I was supposed to jump in and then dance! - without me, no one could ask me to do that - I'm not fucking crazy!

I once saw on television how the Polynesians walk over glowing lava on a ritual, religious occasion. But first of all, this was no lava, secondly, by God I am not a Polynesian and thirdly I am certainly not a crazy Swami with Yogic powers! Every cell in me resisted, common sense appealed to reason - do not do it! Let the Swami think what he wants because of me, I am not obliged to this guy in any way. Let him dance for all, I don't care, preferably all night long until his feet are charred.

Another voice said, "Eno, jump over your shadow. Let your courage prevail over your fear. Do something extraordinary, unconventional, that goes against all rules."

For quite some time I stood in front of the hot embers, struggled with myself, did not know what I wanted, did not know what I should do...

The Swami was chanting *Om* fervently all the time at full throat, so that it was vibrating. Slowly my oppressive fear gave way, my doubt evaporated. I heard only the *Om*, saw only the glow. My mind ceased to exist.

What I did then, was somehow no longer me, it was a part of me that I didn't know until now - when I think about it today, I ask myself how I had the courage at that time.

I bowed before the embers, put my palms together for a greeting and said: "Dear dead man, I ask for your permission to dance on your fire in your ashes. Lord Shiva, with your permission, I enter the sacred fire."

I did a short leap over the trident and landed in the middle of the glowing carpet. There I turned around my own axis, danced so that the glow sparkled and splashed. The whole world was glowing, burning brightly. I merged with fire, became fire myself. In that moment I understood - even if my body would burn - my mind, my consciousness would live on. Again, I turned on my own axis, looked at the sky...It was raining embers.

On the horizon, where sea and sky meet, I saw Shiva and Parvati shining blue-silvery, surrounded by Krishna, Brahma, Ganesh and other holy gods. They all seemed sublime, beautiful, unattainable. Parvati radiated a sex appeal in a way that only women of the gods can. - I was electrified!

Once again, I turned around my own axis like a dervish, splashing, bursting and popping fireworks all around me. I crushed and trampled the demons of fear that the sparks were flying under my feet. I thanked the Gods for having revealed themselves to me, clenched my hand to a fist and shouted, "*Hasta la victoria siempre. Viva la revoluçion*", into the night sky. Then I jumped out of the fire with one leap, back onto the sandy ground.

The Swami hugged me - he had wet eyes.

"Eno", he shouted, "you danced like mad, pure ecstasy - even the Gods applauded!"

"Wow, Swami", I gasped out of breath, "thanks for the credit. I don't dare to look at my feet at all, maybe I'm only standing on two charred stumps in front of you - at best we'll have a foot sole steak for lunch today."

"It's all still there", the Swami reassured me. "Eno, I saw who you really are. When dancing on the fire, everyone is the essence of oneself. The fire forces everyone to take off one's masks. The true expression of the personality can be seen purely and clearly for a few moments."

"What did you see at my place, Swami?"

"Eno, you come from very far away. Your home is a different one You're an alien on Terra. Often you feel lonely because of it, not quite belonging to it all. No doubt you have special abilities and gifts. You are still young, these abilities, these gifts will develop and take effect as you get older."

"What are these gifts and abilities, Swami?"

"The Great Spirit will tell you at the right time, it is too early now - things must mature and grow."

Only now did I dare to look down at my feet - they were both still there, but felt a little warm. A slight pain stung the left sole of my foot, which worried me a little. I sat down to examine the soles of my feet in the glow of the embers. They looked pretty black and charred - at least they didn't smell like a steak, I thought. On closer examination it turned out fortunately, that they were only full of discolored coal and ashes - I was reassured. Only on the left sole of my foot I had a very small blister, which was hardly worth mentioning.

"Are you okay?" asked the Swami.

"It's okay, dude!"

"Then let's go swimming, Eno - steel must be tempered while it still glows!"

Slowly the day began to grey, we went to the beach. I slipped into the sea, under a crest of waves, surfaced, screaming an ardent "Yeaah", into the vastness of the sea. After the hot fire the water felt like cool balm...Gradually the violet-orange sun emerged majestically from the sea - a new day in India...What a mad night I had, unbelievable!

After a morning shower on the rice field we visited Amukaram's food stable, where we ate some *Idlis* and *Puris*. As I became satiated, I slowly felt the tiredness coming on. I was looking forward to sleeping under the tree all day. Apparently, the Swami was in a similar mood.

"I can't wait for my bed", he moaned, "two free nights in two days, I've have enough. When I get home, I'm gonna hit the sack, and the world can kiss my ass."

At the fruit stand we bought two Papayas and a Pineapple. Afterwards we went back to our tree. Through the leaves we could observe how some family members of the deceased had returned to the cremation site. They all sang a song together. Then the widow of the deceased opened a coconut and splashed the water over the still hot ashes that it hissed. Two other women laid a clay plate with food on the floor to the side of the deceased's head.

"The last breakfast", explained the Swami.

With a wooden stick the son of the deceased searched for remnants in the still hot ashes. He wrapped the unburnt pieces of bones he found in a cloth and buried them in the earth a few steps away from the fireplace.

The ritual was finished, the family of the deceased was moving away towards the village. A straying dog, which had probably been waiting for exactly that, made himself over the *last breakfast* with relish and trolled away afterwards - the dead man finally had his peace and so did we! Finally, the longed sleep, I felt dead tired and drained, the last three days had been very intense and exhausting.

In the late afternoon we were woken by hammering noises. The cremator had come back and was about to dismantle the lying bier with a machete. He tied the bamboo and wooden parts onto the luggage rack of his bicycle. Afterwards he made a short visit under our tree. The cremator and the Swami were talking in Tamil, I could not understand a word.

For dinner I got us two portions of *Dal* and some Chapatis at Amukaram's. It became a calm, quiet, contemplative evening. None of us seemed to be all that communicative. At the moment there was nothing to talk about either, it seemed as if everyone was working on his own, in his own world of thoughts, to process the last three days. Soon we laid down to sleep again.

"Good night Swami, sleep well, I hope no one else dies here so soon – I have enough for a while."

But I should have been mistaken...Two days later the cremator brought a lot of wood again. He seemed very tense today, radiating a harsh, aggressive, unapproachable cold.

"I've never seen such an expression on him! Eno, I think for now we better stay under the tree, let him do his work. Something tragic must have happened. Maybe a family member died or a close friend."

Without coming to our tree, he left after the work was done.

Towards evening, a procession of about forty men moved to the cremation site. Six of the men were carrying a very large, flower-decorated bier. Between all the flowers I saw three small, white elongated balls of fabric.

Worried, with pressed lips I looked at the Swami. He had become noticeably paler, his facial expressions frozen - we sensed bad things coming towards us.

"Oh, Swami, oh my God - these are children, three children! Wow, Swami, now it gets very hard, it's gonna be really tough. - I don't know if I can take that...I think this is too much for me. I guess I'll go into town and stay in a hotel for a night or two."

"Eno, I have already experienced a lot of brutal things in India and at this place, what follows here now, surpasses everything that has happened before and deeply shakes my old Swami heart!

Eno, our destiny has brought us to this place. You are here to have exactly these experiences. Both our fates have willed it so. There's little point in running away. It would be cowardly! We both have to face this test!"

In the meantime, the men had put the three children's corpses on the stake and covered them with wood.

The Swami and I wondered what could be the reason for three dead children all at once - some accident seemed the most plausible.

The whole mourning society seemed somehow aggressive, angry and upset. The Swami seemed to be very concerned, I also did not feel very comfortable in my skin.

"Eno, I'm going to pull myself together, I will go and see what's going on...you stay under the tree for now. The situation is somewhat delicate. It looks like some of the men had a lot of *Arak* brandy. In India, such a mood can quickly change, it can lead to turmoil. The one cop with his *Lhati-stick* can't do much about it."

The Swami went to the cremation place. Through the leaves I watched as he greeted some men, talked to them and discussed. He also exchanged a few words with the policeman and the cremator. After a while the Swami returned under our tree with a deadly serious face. "Eno, you can't imagine the tragedy that has happened. Imagine...a mother killed herself and her three children - poisoned! Two boys and a girl, seven, nine and ten years old.

The reason for this act was that her husband had filed for divorce and wanted to marry another woman."

I was shocked, said nothing more!

Never in my live, I had heard something like this before. It was inconceivable But in India the inconceivable, the unthinkable is reality!

We watched as the father of the deceased children lit the cremation fire. He looked absolutely ashamed and pitiful, his knees trembled, he almost threatened to collapse. Two men supported him. I felt no pity for him. Because two adults acted so heartlessly, so coldly, so scrupulously, three innocent children had to die so cruelly. I felt hate and anger towards the parents - I mourned for the children!

Since the relatives, fathers, uncles, grandfathers, brothers-in-law of both parents were present, the tension was literally in the air.

Luckily... the cremation went without incident, the policeman looked sad, but relieved.

After an hour all the men left, my tension eased somewhat, but the sadness remained.

The cremator sat alone by the fire for a while and then came under to our tree, he looked frozen. He sat down with us, we were all silent, nobody spoke a word... Suddenly it broke out of him...the cremator cried heart breaking. I've never seen a man crying like that! The Swami and I cried with him – And I've never seen three men crying together!!!

After a while he began to complain and curse bitterly. He cursed the children's parents, his bleak life, his work. He cursed India, the government, God and the whole world. I do not speak Tamil, but I understood him one hundred percent, every word! In such extreme situations, you understand all languages...

Shortly after the cremator had said goodbye, I laid down on my mat and rolled myself into the blanket. Despite twenty-five degrees heat I was feeling cold. My eyes closed heavy as lead, I just wanted to step down and forget everything.

In the morning about twenty women came to the cremation site. They brought the *last breakfast* for the children - it was heartbreaking! In contrast to the men yesterday, the women let their feelings and emotions ran freely. The Swami and I cried with them.

The rest of the day we spent in silence and sadness, we were paralyzed, feeling broken and exhausted.

In the evening the cremator and two helpers came back to the ground and cremated the mother of the three children. Not a single mourner was present. We also did not show up. The cremator did his job without emotion and soon left again. The fire had a completely different character than yesterday, it seemed cold and lonely. The next morning, a lead-heavy, grey aura lay over the cremation site - from then on, I avoided the fireplace and gave it a wide curve.

I felt like having morning walk alone on the beach. The Swami was still sleeping. About three miles down the beach there were some tourist bungalows and a small restaurant - I could have some breakfast there.

Barefoot, always close to the water, where the last whitecap dries up in the sand, I strolled along the beach. The fire dancing and the cremations had not passed me by without leaving a trace, that all left its mark on me! I needed a moment of distance, of solitude to digest all this...

The beach restaurant was just about to open - I was the first guest. Apparently, the travelers were all still in their feathers. I ordered a milk-coffee and a banana porridge. Because I was so hungry, I ordered a fruit salad afterwards. There was nothing edifying in the newspaper, the usual political blah-blah, wars, terror, disasters... absolutely nothing pleasant.

In the meantime, the restaurant was getting populated with guests. The people showed the typical picture of the traveler and backpacker scene. Swiss German was spoken at the table next to mine. Three boys from Zurich had settled down there and occupied the table with maps, writing pads, cameras and diaries. The waiter had trouble finding a place for the drinks and the food. For a moment I thought about sitting down at their table - speaking Swiss German after a long time - but then I let it stay. I didn't feel like answering the usual tourist questions. After all, what could I tell them? That I just came from a cremation with three children, that I live under a tree and danced on the fire? I lived in a world they probably didn't understand. I, for my part was not particularly interested in their world.

Then Caterina entered the restaurant.

"Hello, Caterina, good to see you, what are you doing in this area at this hour?"

"Good morning, Eno, I've just come from a sick call, a Frenchman who lives here in one of the bungalows stepped into the shards of a broken bottle on the beach yesterday, while jogging, he got it badly, I just pulled out the last splinter of glass. The wound has stopped bleeding, I don't think it need to be stitched, I just hope it doesn't get infected, otherwise we'll have the salad! There is nothing with walking around at the moment, he lies on his bed with his leg high up. I'll get him some crutches tomorrow. The owner of the faci-lity here is a friend of mine, he calls me whenever a tourist has an illness, disease or an injury."

"I think you have a great vocation, Caterina, I'm very impressed. Your way of life is very admirable! Do you actually want to live here in India forever or return to England sometime?"

"I have lived here in India for almost three years now, nothing is pulling me away at the moment. I love this country. I am happy here - every day more. Here I can be as I really am. I have a very special access to the Indian women, they are the ones I love most and the children!"

I told Caterina about the fire dancing and the two cremations, especially the last one with the three children. Caterina was stunned and shocked.

"This is the other side of India...it is at times brutal and merciless. You would like to leave...but already on the next day or next hour some wonderful event full of love, sublimity, magic and beauty happens to you...you are touched and moved and you feel connected with the Creator and the world. India reconciles you again and again! Otherwise it would be unbearable! In India you will find the most stinking cloaks in the world but also the sweetest fragrances in the world, often a few steps apart. You have to accept one for the other, both extremes.

By the way, Eno, I was planning stopping by under your tree anyway. On Saturday an Indian friend of mine is having her wedding party. On this occasion, an Indian Beatles-cover band will play on the roof of the *Roof Garden* restaurant. I'm really excited, almost like the real Beatles are performing. I wanted to ask you and the Swami if you'd like to come along?"

"Wow, Caterina, an Indian Beatles-cover band, I wouldn't miss this, a little of variety is always good. I'm sure the Swami will join us. I know he likes the Beatles very much."

"Okay...then I'll come by your home next Saturday late afternoon. We can have dinner at the wedding, I know there will be a big buffet."

While paying at the counter, I discovered a fragrant, fresh chocolate cake under a fly bonnet. I let wrapping two pieces of it then I made my way back home.

The sun jet was much higher in the sky than on the away, it was quite hot. Sweating and thirsty, I reached our tree, where I first flush down two big glasses of lime water. The Swami sat on his mat, reading in the biography of Sri Aurobindo, which I had bought a few days ago.

"Hello, Swami, old man, good morning, up already? I have to take a shower and refresh myself a little, please watch out for the chocolate cake so that the ants don't get it."

The Swami lifted his head in bewilderment and made big eyes.

"You must be joking, Eno – there's no chocolate cake in India! I ate the last one ten years ago in Kathmandu."

"No kidding, Swami, I just took a walk on the beach to the traveler bungalows. In the restaurant there they had a huge chocolate cake in the display case, I thought I'd bring us two pieces."

The water literally ran together in the Swami's mouth.

"Eno, you're great! While you take a shower, I'll get us a thermos flask of fresh coffee at Amukaram's."

"Great, Swami, a decent coffee, would be great. In the restaurant they had only this instant coffee and it was quite thin - one cup for five Rupees, imagine! At Amukaram's we get for the same money a whole pot full of the best fresh bean coffee - there you see once again how the tourists are getting ripped off."

About half a dozen women worked on the rice paddy today. The water pump was already running, I only had to stand under it. The pump was slightly hidden behind some bushes, so the field workers didn't notice too much of me. Because I had forgotten my terry cloth, I sat down on a slightly elevated slope after the shower, to let myself dry in the sun. The field workers were busy, using hand hoes to optimize the water channels so that the water was distributed evenly over the entire field.

Suddenly one of the women started moaning, bedding in pain. All the other women now interrupted their work and hurried to the one arched in pain.

I thought "What's wrong with her - a cobra bite, maybe a colic or some other industrial accident?"

The groaning woman was now supported by two women on each side, left and right. It was only now that I noticed that she was high pregnant. I slowly realized that this was not a cobra bite or an accident, but the contractions of an impending birth. The pregnant woman moaned and pressed, one woman held up her *sari*, another massaged her belly, a third waited for the baby to come out with a cloth. Apparently, it was not time yet, the pregnant woman became calmer again, until after a few minutes the contractions started again...All of a sudden everything went very fast, it gone *plop,* so to speak...and the new citizen of the earth *plopped* into the *jumping sheet,* which was kept ready...after a few seconds the first cry was heard. I could see one of the women biting through the umbi-lical cord with her teeth and knotting the rest. Gesticulating and laughing, the whole group of women, supporting the young mother, left for the village.

I was quite astonished - how easy it all went, how natural, how fast, without any aids or high-tech. It seemed more logical to give birth in a standing position than lying in a birthing chair - the babies slipped out much better due to their own weight. No man was present at the birth, this was exclusively a woman's matter!

The stray dog, which had already eaten the *last breakfast* of the dead man, now also made a fuss about the afterbirth including the umbilical cord. At first, I wanted to throw a stone, but then I let it stay. If not the dog, the ants or crows eat it - nature wastes nothing!

India always reconciles you! - As Catherina said. After the cremation of the three children, the experience of birth brought reconciliation.

Back under the tree the Swami was waiting for me impatiently.

"You took a hell of a long shower, Eno! You're lucky that the two pieces of cake are not cleaned up yet, that I could control myself - to put an old man on the rack like that!"

Inward I had to laugh, I knew the Swami had a weakness for sweets. And as he stood there, he seemed to me like a little boy who now wanted his cake. We sat down on our mats, the Swami poured the coffee into the cups, I unpacked the cake. Silently we munched the chocolate cake and drank the coffee with it. The Swami enjoyed the cake as only one can, who hadn't eaten any for ten years, but only dreamed of it.

"By the way, Swami, I met Caterina – There's a wedding party on Saturday at the Roof-Garden, an Indian Beatles-cover band is playing, we're both invited, are you coming too?"

"Yeah, man! I am the biggest Beatles fan on this planet... Obladiobladaaa... Yesterdaaay... Let it beeee..."

The Swami sang a Beatles medley, clapped his hands, rejoiced like a child.

When he seemed a bit calmer again and his senses were no longer limited to cake and the Beatles, I told him about the birth in the rice field.

"What I am experiencing and going through here, Swami, is quite crazy! I have never felt so shaken in my life. The last few days have been extremely intense. I hope my brain can withstand all these impressions and experiences without burning out."

"Remember, Eno, a few weeks ago you asked me if I am not bored just sitting under the tree? As you can see for yourself, there is always a lot going on here. By the way, it is a good sign that you have experienced a birth after so much death. The cycle is now closed - the "Great Spirit" means it very well with you!"

"What do you mean, Swami? Sometimes I have the impression that you control the story and already know how it ends."

"Well, it's not that easy", the Swami replied. "In any case, everything happens for your own good. You play a special role in a special film - the director is the Great Spirit!"

"That could be fun! What do you think I see next in this amazing film...?"

In the evening, when I went to Amukaram's to get dinner for us, I had a very tragic encounter: Out of the shade of the trees, a young, ragged woman suddenly stepped towards me with a baby in her arms. Wildly gesticulating and whining she held the child towards me. I couldn't understand exactly what she was saying. However, from her expressions and gestures I ga-thered after a while, that she wanted to sell me the baby for one hundred Rupees!

This could not be true - a mother wanted to sell her own child for three dollars! Outraged and indignant I waved away. The woman started to moan and cry even more. I tried to reassure her, to make it clear to her, that she could not simply sell her child for a hundred Rupees - but what did I know about the plight of these people! Now she even started to go down with the price, eighty Rupees, fifty Rupees, twenty Rupees. I got really angry and yelled at her. The infant began to cry.

I was in total emotional chaos! A mixture of anger, pity, disgust and endless love for this little child!

Suddenly the woman pushed the baby into my arms and ran away. There I stood, alone in India, with a newborn in my arms which did not belong to me.

Gently I put the baby down on the floor and ran after the woman. It had become almost dark in the meantime, the terrain was impassable, full of cacti and bushes. I lost sight of her in the darkness, the night simply swallowed her. So I went back to the crying baby, picked it up and tried to calm it down with a gentle voice - a wave of protective instinct hormones was floating through me. What should I do now, with the infant, go to Amukaram or back to the Swami? Somehow, I felt the need to show the little one to the Swami, so I decided to go back to the tree. The swinging movements while walking calmed the baby, it stopped crying - that was already half of the rent, my nervousness subsided a little.

"Hi, Swami, dude, we gonna have to postpone our dinner, I just have received a baby." The Swami swallowed empty and looked at me in wonder. His stunned expression made me laugh out loud. The situation was somehow tragic, grotesque and funny at the same time. I could hardly stand on my feet because of all the laughter and handed the little one over to the Swami. He pulled his face, like Charlie Chaplin after the thrown cake in his face. I was crumbling over with laughter. The last days had not been very funny, so this laughter had a very liberating and releasing effect. Also, the Swami started to laugh out loud. The little one looked astonished with big eyes and smiled brightly. My heart was melting. For a short sequence, all three of us were happy. There was no past, no future, there was only this one moment of the present in unconditional love.

"Swami, I'm keeping the little one! I feed it with rice milk, coconut milk and vegetable gruel, I am sure there is a nurse in the village who has some breast milk left. I don't care if it's a boy or a girl – this is a problem of fucking India! This is a collective crime! And one day they have to pay the bill - I can't believe they created the law of Karma?!" – I was very angry and upset!!!

"Eno, Eno, you have a big heart! I actually believe you'd go through with it. I too would like to keep the little one. Half a year ago, I already faced this situation together with Lisa. We went to eat at Amukaram's, back at the tree, there was a foundling underneath. After the first shock Lisa was blown away. I too saw myself as a grandfather. But we both had to realize with a heavy heart that it was not possible to keep the child. Lisa lived illegally in India. Her tourist visa had expired years ago. I also had no documents. In the end we took the child to an orphanage with a heavy heart.

"What kind of orphanage is this, Swami, is it clean and friendly there?"

"It is a Christian orphanage, with white-dressed sisters, very clean for Indian standards. There is a peaceful, beautiful atmosphere, I think the children are doing well. Lisa and I visit our foundling once a month, -we have named it Suraja - I am very happy each time."

"Ok, Swami, we will go up to the street with the child and drive with a rickshaw to this orphanage - it will be hungry and thirsty soon, we have to hurry a little bit, we have to change the diapers before!

I got one of my old *lungis,* that I had washed yesterday and tore it into a diaper and three washcloths. The Swami held the child up, I removed the old cloth diaper, which was wet, rotten and dirty - only now I was one hundred percent sure that it was a girl. I washed the little one underneath with the wet washcloths and put the new orange diaper on her.

The little girl behaved amazingly calm, she panted and gurgled once and kicked a little with her legs.

Finally, we covered her with a cloth and headed for the road, the Swami in front with a flashlight, me in the back with the baby in my arms. Halfway down the line, the girl started to cry.

"Swami, she's hungry and thirsty. What are we to do?"

"We go to Amukaram, he has two babies, maybe his wife has something left."

Amukaram and his wife Usha were amazed but reacted very calmly. After the Swami had briefly explained how we had come to the child, Usha handed the little one to her own breast. Our little girl immediately found the connection and desirably sucked the milk. After she was saturated, it seemed quite content and happy, she even smiled - our hearts melted.

We stopped a rickshaw and let the three of us chauffeured to the St. Thomas Children Home. After a short drive the little girl had already fallen asleep, the loud engine didn't seem to bother her at all.

"Swami, the little girl needs a name, I don't want to just hand her over in anonymously. It's a human being, it's not just a package in the post office! Do you know a beautiful Indian girl's name?"

"Aisha?"

"Aisha, sounds good, Swami, a very beautiful name."

"Ok...little girl, listen carefully", I whispered into her ear, "we are not your parents, we are not even related to you, we are just two crazy guys with a big heart. In the name of Shiva and all Indian gods we baptize you in the name of Aisha." I gave her a little kiss to the forehead...Aisha was baptized.

After half an hour of driving we reached the St. Thomas Children Home, where we could hand over the still sleeping little Aisha to the head nurse. She reacted very friendly and understanding. Because the Swami was acquainted with the head nurse, the handover of the little Aisha went smoothly and without bureaucracy, we did not even have to fill out a form or provide a signature. (Aisha now lives in *Auroville*, is married to a German born in *Auroville* and has two children. - The little girl has made her way despite a difficult start. She has become a very beautiful woman. and works part-time in an *Auroville* boutique and leads a harmonious family life - I am very proud of her!)

We were lucky, Amukaram had not yet closed his food stable, so we could eat a little something there on the way back. During the meal I told the Swami how I once saved a little girl from suffocation in the Peruvian jungle. It was like this:

"After a long day's walk, with machetes and heavy backpacks loaded with food for a week, Jan and I made our way through the impassable Peruvian jungle, reaching the *Rio Yuyapichis*, where we thought we would wash gold with the gold pans we had brought with us.

Completely unexpectedly we discovered, close to the riverbank, three half-decayed, uninhabited huts made of boards and bamboo, covered with corrugated iron roofs. The largest of the huts stood on two-meter-high stilts - Oh, how practical - so we did not have to build a camp - in the stilt house we could sleep protected from dangerous predators. Mostly we were afraid of Jaguars.

In the two huts on the ground there was an unbelievable, garbage-like chaos. Half-rotten clothes, blankets, decaying furniture, broken shelves, broken dinnerware and a huge number of different medicine, pills, tablets tubes and bottles in half-rotten original packaging. The name *Dr. Koepcke* was written everywhere on the yellowed, damp, half-eaten books, dossiers and files. After we had examined and rummaged through all the junk, a puzzle picture slowly crystallized.

We had discovered *Dr. Koepcke's* abandoned jungle research station by pure coincidence...And that Doctor *Koepcke* was not an unknown person!

In the early 1970s an airplane crashed over the Peruvian jungle. Nearly one hundred people were killed. As if by a miracle, *Juliane Koepcke*, the seventeen-year-old daughter of the doctor, was the only person, who survived this accident slightly injured. Juliane's mother was also killed by that crash.

For ten days the brave girl fought, without food along a river through the jungle, until she accidentally arrived at an Indian camp, completely speckled by mosquito bites. The Indians provided first aid and then brought her to a hospital in Pucallpa.

This survival story went through the entire world press at that time. There is even a book and a cinema film about it.

Unbelievable! we had actually discovered by chance in this huge Amazon forest of South America the abandoned jungle research station of *Dr. Koepcke*, the *Panguana*...

On the second day, after we had settled in the stilt house, we tried gold panning. The work was extremely strenuous and laborious, we did not really master the technique. In addition, dozens of small fish swam around our bare feet, nibbling off our corneas, the smaller ones tickled us and the larger ones tweaked...it was not to endure! Exasperated, we gave up gold panning after two hours. We hadn't found any gold, but for this we had super clean and shiny feet.

And now, Swami, comes the rescue story: One evening, just before it got dark, a canoe moored on the river bank at our place. On board, mother, father and their little daughter of about one year. The little one seemed to have great difficulty with breathing, almost got no air and rattled. The Indios told us that the little girl swallowed a leech which had now docked in her throat, soaked itself full with blood and became thicker and thicker. The kid was almost choking... Wow...that was strong tobacco!

The Indios hoped and asked us desperately if we could help them in any way?

I forgot my watery eyes and my pity - quick action was now the order of the day. A huge adrenalin rush shot through my body. Jan as well was in three seconds awake...Emergency case!

Father and mother now held the kicking child by the arms and legs. Jan shone with a flashlight. I tried to open the little girl's mouth, which hardly succeeded, the girl had an incredibly strong bite, refused to open her mouth and shook her head like crazy. In addition, it was impossible to penetrate the small child's mouth with two fingers. The first four milk teeth did not make things easier. My index finger was bitten almost to the bone.

Suddenly it occurred to me that I had an industrial tweezer in my luggage, seven inches long, angled at the front, fortunately not pointed but rounded. I sprinted to the stilt house, got the tweezer out of my luggage.

Now the father fixed the head of the child between the knees and held the arms. The mother held her legs. Jan shone the flashlight. Now I tried again to open the small mouth and to push the tweezer inside, which was more or less successful. But the little one, however, bit on the tweezer so that her teeth crunched on the metal, anyway I couldn't see anything because her mouth was closed.

Suddenly I had an intuition, my technical school and education came to my aid.

"Jan, we need a piece of bamboo cane, about one inch long and one and a half inch in diameter, hollow inside." Jan immediately understood what I was up to. In no time at all he looked for a suitable bamboo cane, pulled his survival dagger, which was equipped with a saw, and sawed the appropriate part in a few seconds. The little girl could hardly breathe no more, had no longer strength to defend herself. I could easily push the cane part into her mouth, it fitted like a glove, the tongue lay nicely under the bamboo piece, I had a clear path!

"Eno, if this doesn't work, I have a plan B, then I'll use a razor blade to make a *tracheotomy*. I know where and how to do it...a cross-cut just above the collarbone below the throat," - That Jan...wow, pretty cold-blooded - I was amazed...from where he knew this so well? While Jan fetched a razor blade and sterilized it with a lighter, I shone with the flashlight through the bamboo tube into the girl's throat. The visibility was better than I had thought...There, clearly, I could see something black and slippery in the back of the throat, which obviously didn't belong there.

Now I led the tweezer gently through the hole of bamboo cane and got this horror leech already at the first attempt between the forceps. Very slowly I pulled the tweezer back, I could clearly feel a resistance, it was as if I was pulling on a rubber band. Suddenly it went *plop*... and this disgusting leech was outside.

The little girl took a huge deep breath, the whole chest inflated. The parents got down on their knees and prayed. Jan and I hugged each other with wet eyes. -It was done!

We were both glad we didn't have to use Plan B. -But I'm sure Jan would have removed it without hesitation. Unbelievable! Jan was only nineteen years old at the time and I was twenty. Jan was a damned daring and cool guy for his age. Without him I would have been lost in the jungle, would have lost my orientation. Self-confident and without fear he stomped through the rainforest as if he had been born there. For my part, I no longer knew where back and front or north and south were. When I asked him desperately every now and then, whether he still had the orientation, he always said, in a self-confident tone: "Of course...this is the way, the sun stands over there!' For my part, I had no idea where the sun had risen or where it was going to set.

Well...I surrendered to the situation and just trusted him...I knew instinctively, he's got it!

Our whole rescue action had lasted about twenty minutes, it seemed like an eternity to us. When the father of Rosa, that was the girl's name, wanted to offer us some money, we refused with thanks and determination. But when he offered us a cigarette, we took it warmly, because we had run out of tobacco for two days - it was the best cigarette of my life!

Jan and I invited the exhausted family to stay with us in the stilt house. With thanks they accepted our offer. - For that night, we were one family. I couldn't fall asleep for a long time, the adrenalin level and the happiness hormones had to subside first.

In the morning the Indio family said goodbye to us. Rosa, the little girl, sucked on her mother's breast, smacking her lips and looked contentedly, you could not imagine that just a few hours ago she was in grave danger.

The Indio family invited us to spend a few days in their village. Because her current canoe was too small for all of us, the father wanted to pick us up the day after next with a bigger canoe. Because Jan's visa for Peru was about to expire and he had to return to Lima, he unfortunately could not accept this invitation. For my part, I was faced with the choice of doing this trip alone. It was a difficult decision but somehow, I didn't feel like saying goodbye to Jan so suddenly in the next ten minutes.

The Indio family boarded their canoe and took off. When little Rosa smiled at us at the farewell, our hearts were aching. A part of me would have loved to go with them - maybe I would still live happily in that Indio village by the river, in the rain forest - maybe I would have been spared a lot of things...

Jan and I took off back the next day. A day's march through the jungle to a small village, from where we started our expedition. We checked in to a small pension, a wooden hut with a corrugated iron roof and a neon tube - it was absolutely dreary. We planned to fly back to Pucallpa with the same Cessna and the bush pilot we had already come with. There was no road connection. The plane or a boat on the river were the only external connection. So, we sat all day long on the riverbank waiting for the sound of the Cessna's engine or a boat passing by. In the evening we were still sitting there. The Indios put us off on *Manana*. For dinner we had beans with fried eggs, that was the only thing you could get. For breakfast we had beans with boiled eggs. After waiting all morning at the river bank, we had beans with scrambled eggs for lunch. And in the evening of course again beans with fried eggs. Nothing could be found in the village except eggs and beans. There wasn't even a piece of bread. After five days we were still squatting on the river bank, waiting and eating beans and eggs three times a day - it was grueling! In the evening we bought a bottle of *Pisco* brandy, which was the only thing you could get besides eggs and beans, we sat down on the shore, smoked Inca cigarettes and drank the whole bottle away. Late at night we swayed roaring into our dreary wooden sheds. The first thing I saw after I turned on the light...was a big black tarantula sitting on the floor next to the bed - Oh, my God... and this one too - drunk as a skunk with a tarantula?! After I had chased this creature through the whole room cursing, I finally managed to crush this monster...Brrr...The other day after our hangover breakfast of eggs and beans, we were sitting again waiting at the river bank. We were surprised that nobody was fishing because of this monotonous and meagre food. When we asked the locals, they simply said, *Pescado no*...and when we asked for a boat or a ship, they said, *Mañana*. It was grueling!

Two days later we finally heard the engines of an airplane...It was our Cessna which flew us half an hour over the jungle to Pucallpa! On board a fat Indio lady with ten chickens in a wooden box. In Pucallpa there was finally a culinary change. We had been on a very monotonous and poor diet for the last three weeks. The noodles with minced meat sauce and a bottle of beer, seemed like a dish from another world.

Jan and I stayed another two days in Pucallpa, then we went separate ways. As a farewell present he gifted me his *jungle bayonet* which I still own today.

Unfortunately, my address book was stolen later on in India and I was never able to contact him. And I forget his surname. I suppose that his address book has also been lost somehow, otherwise he would certainly have contacted me once. (At that time in 1979, there were no smartphones and mobile phones) - I would give a lot to know what happened to him, to see him again. I hope he has a comfortable life.

My jungle friend Jan from Germany, I have never forgotten him!

This story Swami, I have never told to anyone, not to a girlfriend and not to a friend, you are the first person I tell it to."

"I'm very honored, Eno, that was an extraordinary, thrilling story, you don't get stories like that at the regulars table..."

Back under the tree, we laid down immediately on the mats, dead tired, after this eventful day. But like it is sometimes, I had trouble falling asleep. Aisha and Rosa were still too present at the moment.

Because I didn't had anything suitable to wear for the wedding party, I drove back to the city the next morning to get an adequate outfit - whoever could afford the Beatles on the Roof-Garden was certainly part of the Indian upper class, it wasn't necessarily appropriate to enter there with worn out plastic slippers, out frayed shorts and an old washed up T-shirt. So, I went to a boutique and bought myself some cool royal blue pants, a leather belt, and a yellow shirt with collar. In a shoe shop I bought a pair of black shoes with silver buckles and a pair of white socks.

After the shopping I went to a bar and had a bottle of Kingfisher beer and reviewed the last days - after the second bottle I was quite melancholic and suddenly dog-tired, which was no wonder after all the *events* of the last time. I would have loved to order a third bottle and slowly drink myself under the table - that was not my style at all, but at the moment I didn't care about anything - I just wanted to sleep and forget!

I pulled myself together, paid the bill, sat in a rickshaw and drove back to our tree. There I immediately hit the mat and slept deeply for several hours. The Swami, as well contrary to his habits, took an extended afternoon nap. The last few days had been very hard for him too - I was astonished the whole time anyway, what this eighty-two years old Swami could endure and went through. He had a remarkable physical condition and vitality for his age.

"If I wouldn't do my yoga exercises every morning, I would be an old, weak, bent man on a stick", he said - I didn't doubt his statement for a second!

Finally, it had become Saturday, I was really looking forward to the Beatles-cover concert, I could not wait for it until evening. The Swami as well was looking forward to it very much, was impatient like a child.

In the late afternoon I showered extensively and washed my hair, then I slipped into my newly bought clothes. After all these weeks going barefoot, the socks and new shoes felt strangely tight and stiff. Last but not least, due to lack of hair gel, I put some egg protein in my hair and formed a cool hairstyle.

The Swami marveled at my transformation. He'd never seen me in a look like this before.

For this festive occasion he also put on a new orange *lunghi* and a black gilet. He tied his dreadlocks into a *Shiva knot* over his head - he looked splendid!

Then, in the evening, Caterina came to pick us up. She had also dressed festively, wearing a tight Punjabi dress made of a mixture of turquoise and purple silk, trimmed with golden embroidery, on her feet gold-colored sandals. She had made a discreetly make up today - her resemblance to Nefertiti was striking!

"Hello Nefertiti", I greeted her, "you look absolutely stunning and enchanting today - compliments!"

"Likewise, Eno, wow...you look like Akhenaton in his business look and you Swami like the risen Socrates in a Sunday dress."

So, we marveled at each other for a while, joking together, then we made our way to the village - the Swami with his trident!

In the village we caused quite a stir, everyone was amazed with open mouths and shouted: "Oh...ah and hey." Around Caterina the women gathered, all praising her beauty and wanting to feel the fabric of her dress.

Because there was no room for the long trident in the rickshaw, the Swami had to hold it out of the window at an angle towards the top. On the way, Caterina dug a pre-rolled joint out of her handbag, which the three of us smoked. Afterwards we were in a really good mood, joking and laughing our heads off. For a policeman we passed, apparently it was quite normal that there was a trident looking out of the rickshaw three-foot high. Even the traffic policeman, who stood on a pedestal as the spikes passing in front of his nose, did not bat an eyelid – Shiva's trident seemed to be taboo.

At the Roof-Garden the wedding party was already in full swing. Over a hundred guests stood around in small groups, helped themselves at the buffet or sat on plastic chairs by the edge of the wall. All the people were festively dressed, the women wore expensive silk saris, a few had ventured into Western brand jeans. The men were in starched shirts and polished shoes. The guests all seemed very young and well educated.

Caterina introduced the Swami and me to the bridal couple and gifted them a hand blender as a wedding present, which she had wrapped in golden paper. The two of them were very charming and relaxed, were very happy about the Western visit and the wedding present.

The whole terrace was decorated with garlands and small colorful light bulbs. At the front of the small stage, which was illuminated by a few spots, were three ancient tube amps of indefinable origin and an old, battered drum kit.

After we ate at the rich buffet, the concert started.

The Indian Beatles entered the stage in sixties suits, mushroom hairstyles and slung over guitars.

I was excited - the worn guitars seemed to have had their best times long ago, the dented microphones looked more like projectiles...

But then, wham...the boys got going, with *Sergeant Peppers* as their first song.

From the old speakers the true sixties sound was booming and roaring – that's how the Beatles must have sounded in their early days. I was thrilled - after three months of abstinence from music this sound went through every cell of my body. With the third song, *Back in the USSR,* Caterina and I would have loved to dance off, but we had to pull ourselves together, because we were the only ones. The Indian audience seemed a bit stiff and prudish, their faces radiated joy and enthusiasm, but their bodies could not be moved, a tentative taping with one foot was already the highest of feelings. With the fifth song, *Oh Darling,* I thought - now the place is boiling up - the guitarist played the riff to ecstasy, the drummer didn't seem earthly anymore, the singer gave his whole soul full of fervor...The Indian audience stood there like rooted to the spot. Only the transfigured faces, the bright eyes and the frenetic applause could tell that they were in full swing.

The Swami also went full on, he liked the concert very much, he leaned on his trident, bounced his foot and shook the dreadlocks from time to time.

The band seemed really well-oiled, played very tight and compact. The musicians understood their craft.

It was very warm on the roof terrace, after twenty minutes the polyester jackets of the boys were sweat through, their mushroom hairstyles were hanging down, sweat was dripping from their chins.

After almost two hours the concert of the Indian Beatles was over, the band was shattered and exhausted. After a long thunderous applause, the guys played *Yellow Submarine* and *I am the Walrus* - it was really great! - Cover bands are not really my thing but this was not a usually cover band for me. For me they were the Indian Beatles! And I'm still proud today that I got to see them.

It was Sunday morning, the Swami and I were chilling out, eating breakfast, discussing and talking about this and that.

"How actually, Swami, did life on this planet increase, all this species and biodiversity? A few mosses and lichens cannot produce mushrooms, melons and palms. From a few amino acids, fish, beetles and dinosaurs mutate, and finally humans? Somehow, I miss a link in Darwin's teaching. You once said that coincidence not exist! - so if there is no coincidence, there must be a plan!"

"Right Eno, the Great Spirit has a plan - he is not throwing dice!"

Imagine, Eno, a few billion years ago our earth was a volcanic, glowing lava planet constantly bombarded by comets. These comets consisted mainly dust, rocks and ice. This ice melted on the hot earth, water and steam were created, the steam condensed and rained down. Our planet slowly cooled down, the earth's crust became firmer, water gathered in the deepest places to form lakes and oceans - this is how the water came to our planet. The water we drink every day actually are melted comets.

And now comes the clou, Eno, these ice comets contained certain spores and seeds that germinated and multiplied with the necessary water. But these ice meteorites also transported certain larvae and eggs from which life hatched, which multiplied and developed in water, on land and in the air. When a simple infrastructure and a simple bio-life cycle was created, the earth was visited by extraterrestrial arks which brought the dinosaurs and our primitive animals."

"Why, Swami, were those dinosaurs here and why did they all have to die, what sense does it make?"

"The dinosaurs were very important for the development of the earth, they created a large part of the humus, spread seeds and supplied the plants with nitrogen. Imagine a herd of dinosaurs eating an acre of forest at lunchtime, then hiking ten miles further and shitting out the digested forest again - five tons of compost with undigested seeds which could germinate ideally in this nutrient medium. The dinosaurs inhaled the oxygen that the plants released and breathed the nitrogen that the plants needed. The dinos had big lungs. With two breaths, they converted fifty gallons of oxygen into nitrogen. They created a large part of the primeval atmosphere.

The dinosaurs ruled the earth for a billion years – that's a lot of compost and nitrogen!

The impact of a huge asteroid meant the end of the dinosaurs. The impact caused a gigantic flood wave, which wiped out all life on wide parts of the still new earth. Around the earth a thick cloud of dust formed for years, for a long time the sun could not be seen anymore, it became much cooler. The dinosaurs were cold-blooded, they could not tolerate the low tempe-ratures. In addition, food became scarce, and due to lack of sunlight many of the plants that the dinosaurs ate died or withered. In addition, the thick, dusty air was hard to breathe, their airways and lungs were congested. All these factors meant the end of the area of the dinosaurs. Many of the few primitive mammals survived the catastrophe, they were less temperature-dependent and needed smaller amounts of food. Because their breathing was shallower, had less suction, the nostrils were much smaller and had fine filter hairs, the dusty air was less likely to harm them.

After the earth recovered from this catastrophe, extraterrestrial arks landed again and brought the ancestors of many of our mammals, fish and birds - they also brought the ancestors of modern man.

On the seventh day the Great Spirit contemplated his creation and was satisfied with his work! - The earth was fertilized."

"Wow, Swami, that's a whole new theory of the evolution! I don't know if the scientists, the Pope and Darwin would like that...?"

"With my theory of evolution, there's no question whether the egg or the chicken came first. Our scientists still have no answer to this question.

Life on this planet is of extraterrestrial origin!
The "Great Spirit" fertilizes the universe in his own way!"

After a rich lunch we laid down on the mats and took a nap. Last night had been long, we were both tired. I pondered Swami's theory of evolution a little while, reviewed the Beatles and fell asleep calmly.

Suddenly, it howled, roared, rattled and it made deafening noise, we were really catapulted out of sleep. Sand and leaves flew through the air - we dashed off the mats like feathers, covered our ears with our hands and rushed out from the tree-exit into the open, in panic.

In the sky we saw three Indian military helicopters, which flew one after the other in low level flight just above our treetop. The skids nearly touched the crown. Our tree looked like it was being hit by a hurricane. We nearly got blown away by the wind.

After a few seconds the whole spook was over. Only the buzzard couple was still fluttering around their palm tree, disturbed and excited... a miracle that their nest had stayed up there with the young ones!

"They are completely crazy", shouted the Swami, indignantly with his arms flailing, "to fly so low, they are completely stupid, these idiots!"

I also used some curse words, picked up a stone and threw it towards the helicopters.

When we had calmed down a bit, we went back under our tree. Our clothes, sleeping mats, the dishes, everything was tangled up and flew away, my drinking cup I found after some searching in the branches of the tree.

We couldn't explain why the helicopters were flying so low along the beach - maybe it was an exercise, a maneuver, or maybe the pilots just wanted to have some fun!

"In Los Angeles, Swami, I was once tracked by two police helicopters."

"Oh yes, tell me again one of your American stories, yesterday we didn't get to it because of the Beatles."

"So that's what happened - it's a cool story Swami!"

I lived for some time in Los Angeles, where I worked as a technician in the rocket industry. One weekend, it was late Saturday afternoon, I spontaneously decided to go out of town on my motorbike and spend the night in the mountains. I strapped my sleeping bag and iso-mat onto the bike, spread on some sandwiches, made a thermos flask of coffee, grabbed the remaining two cans of beer from the fridge and drove away from the stuffy, smoggy city, away into the nature.

Slowly leaving the city behind me, I turned up the *Box Canyon*. At a protected place, not visible from the road, I parked my motorcycle. On foot I continued along a small path. The terrain was slightly hilly, overgrown with almost knee-high grass, big boulders and stones laid around everywhere. After a while I passed two lonely houses. Out of one of them a dog barked and yelped like mad. After the houses, the terrain became steeper, rockier, and the footpath slowly got lost. After some search I found a flat, comfortable place on a huge flat boulder, where I decided to spend the night. I unrolled the sleeping mat and sleeping bag, sat cross-legged on it, ate two sandwiches, drank a can of beer, smoked a spliff and enjoyed the silence and peace that surrounded me. In the meantime, it had become dark, the huge, endless sea of lights of Los Angeles was sparkling and glittering. On the horizon it met with the shining sea of stars - it was overwhelming!

In the far distance I saw two helicopters rising. I didn't pay a big attention to them, it was nothing unusual, in L.A. helicopters were flying over the city every day. I suspected they were police helicopters. The two helicopters moved approximately in my direction, became slowly larger and larger. Maybe there was an accident somewhere, a robbery or a car chase. Slowly the helicopters moved out of the inhabited city area towards the Box Canyon, towards to the hills.

Strange... I wondered what they were looking for. There must be something going on nearby - maybe a car accident on the *Box Canyon*? And as I was pondering there, the two helicopters were more or less in low flying over me. Suddenly they turned on their searchlights. The one boulder, a few yards in front of me, was fully illuminated, bright as day - Damn it!? Immediately I grasped the situation - it couldn't be true...I was the reason for their search! - Probably someone from the last two houses, where the dog had been yapping so much, had informed the police and reported that someone was prowling around in the hills. Maybe a convict got away recently, the cops thought they'd see what was going on up there.

Within seconds I stuffed the sleeping bag and the thermos flask into the backpack. With the iso-matt in one hand and the rucksack in the other, I jumped down from my boulder. The helicopters now began to systematically search the whole area with their searchlights. I hastily hid my luggage under a small bush. One of the cones of light moved straight towards the bush. I dove to a boulder, landed there on all fours. Lying on my stomach, I pressed myself to the ground, as close as possible to the rock. The shrub with my things under it, was bathed in bright light. The spotlight missed me by half a yard.

The small boulder did not offer enough cover, I scrambled up, sprinted to some big rocks. Again, a helicopter approached with a deafening howling engine, I had to throw myself to the ground again. This time the outer edge of the light cone grazed me. For two or three seconds I was in the spot light...Shit, now they've seen me! Again, I pulled myself up, ran towards the boulders. Arriving there, a cone of light grazed me again. Now it's over, I thought, but they didn't seem to have discovered me again. Maybe it was because of my brown pants, my gray shirt. But even these rocks did not offer enough cover. Bent, I ran to another group of rocks...I was lucky, three of the rocks laid on top of each other in such a way that a small cave was formed between them, with my feet ahead I crawled into it. There was just enough room for me to crouch there in embryo position. Outside it became daylight, the engines howled, the rotors fluttered, sand whirled into my cave. One of the helicopters hovered exactly over my rock group. Maybe they had seen me before?... After a while, however, the helicopter turned off. - Hopefully they won't land, search the area with police dogs, went through my mind. But none of this happened. For some time, the two helicopters searched the whole area, then they gave up and flew away slowly towards the city. With my eyes I followed them until they disappeared somewhere in the glittering lights of Los Angeles. A stone fell from my heart, I breathed again! For some while I waited, didn't dare to come out of my hiding place...The helicopters didn't come back, everything remained calm. Only then I ventured out of my cave, took out my luggage from under the bush, went back to my lookout point on the boulder. To calm down, I drank the rest of my beer and smoked another spliff. At some point I crawled into my sleeping bag and fell asleep peacefully.

Just at sunrise I woke up, ate my last sandwich, emptied the thermos flask of coffee, enjoyed the sunrise over the still sleeping city. Afterwards I made my way home. Because I was sure that someone had called the police from the last two houses I had passed, I didn't dare to pass them on my way back. But there was no other accessible way to the road, so I had to climb around half of the mountain in a rather daring tour.

Hopefully the cops hadn't discovered my bike, stationed no guard there! With my license plate from Texas I was half suspicious anyway, I didn't have a driver's license either, my tourist visa had expired half a year ago - this could end badly! With a queasy feeling I sneaked back to my bike...Fortunately, there was nobody there, everything seemed to be unharmed. With the first kick the engine started, slowly I drove down the *Box Canyon* - no roadblock, no control, no cop car in the rearview mirror. It was Sunday morning, seven o'clock, there was no traffic on the *Box Canyon* road. But I didn't really feel comfortable until I got into the highway and knew the mountain road behind me - I couldn't have known that the cops would stand on my mat four days later, even if for a completely different reason."

"Wow, that sounds exciting, Eno, tell me!"

"Four days later, when I came home from work in the evening, George, a friend from Switzerland with whom I shared our apartment, was sitting in our living room with two freaky looking guys. - Ah, visitors, I thought, probably work mates, dropping by for a beer after work."

I greeted the two, who introduced themselves as Mike and John, sat down on the still free upholstered chair. I wondered a little why there were no drinks on the table and why George was sitting between the two guys on our little sofa.

"Do you want to smoke a joint?' asked Mike, who was wearing washed out jeans, a faded Hawaiian shirt, tinted sunglasses and greasy, half-long hair.

"Oh yes, gladly', I replied, there is nothing better after a hard day's work!'

Mike pulled a leather case from his breast pocket, which he opened and held out to me. He muttered something about L.A. Narcotic Police. I was a little irritated when I looked at a silver sheriff's star and a tattered ID card, instead of the expected *Rizla Papers.*

The guy is probably kidding me, I thought, I can get such a tin star in any toy store. We're not in the Wild West anymore! It looks like he's trying to scare a European greenhorn.

Unimpressed, I looked at the sheriff's star and said, "What a great joke, man, you can't scare me with that. When I was a little boy, I wore one of those tin stars on my cowboy carnival costume.'

"This is no joke! This is an original sheriff's star and an original police ID card, Mike claimed in a justifiable tone.

"Oh... come on', if you want to do a joke with me, you'll have to do it a bit smarter! Your alleged police ID looks more like an expired public swimming pool subscription!'

The two alleged police officers looked at each other in disbelief. George looked entered. - So, I gave it back to them in a cool way. I thought, they probably think we Europeans are naive!

"What kind of weird guys have you brought with you,' I asked George in Swiss German, "are they your work mates?"

"Eno, you bloody idiot, they're cops, plainclothes drug squads, you understand?!'

"Come on, these two stringy freaks look more like ex-junkies - you three guys have been talking it over", I said in English again, "you want to have fun with me. Stop fooling around – let's have a beer and smoke!"

Somehow, I didn't want to admit the gravity of the situation. Now, John, who hadn't said anything until now, grabbed me by the shoulders, shook me and yelled: "This is no joke, goddammed, this is fucking reality, you understand! We're arresting you both for possession and cultivation of marijuana!"

My friend looked very depressed and serious - it slowly dawned on me that the situation was apparently really serious.

"Where do you hide your weed?", the cop yelled at me again. "You better tell us, or we'll tear this place apart!", he threatened. "Your friend was smart enough to hand over his stuff."

"Over there in the top drawer," I replied, pointing to our commode. The cop opened the drawer and triumphantly took out my plastic bag with a quarter ounce of grass.

"Is that all, or do you have hidden some more somewhere?", he wanted to know.

"That is all," I assured him.

"Cultivating marijuana is severely punished in California," the cop said, pointing to our windowsill, where we had a small flowerpot in the size of a yoghurt cup with a handful of soil and three tiny water shoots barely three inch in size.

Despite the tragedy, I had to laugh inside. You hardly couldn't call these three scalawags, marijuana cultivation...but law enforcement officers are sometimes petty and stubborn! With a scissor, the cop cut off the three tiny creatures, which he provided with a serious expression as *corpus delicti* in a small plastic bag. Now I had to turn around with my face to the wall and hold my hands up, being scanned for weapons...it clicked...and before I knew what's going on, a handcuff snapped and shut on my right wrist. George got the other part of the handcuff around his left wrist. Like that, chained together we were taken away and driven with the police car to the police headquarters.

On the way the cops asked us where we worked and how much money we earned per hour.

"As a technician at Space Vector Cooperation for twelve Dollars an hour," I replied.

"As an electronic engineer at Rockwell International for fifteen Dollars an hour", George replied.

The two cops were visibly impressed and amazed with open mouths, explaining that they only earn ten Dollars an hour. "Not currently overpaid, those L.A. cops", I thought to myself – "for ten bucks an hour in the drug investigation?!"

At that moment, although the cops were sitting at the longer lever, the hierarchical-social position was turning. We were well-trained professionals, worked in international corporations, they were losers in the end, who couldn't think of anything cleverer than arresting peaceful pot smokers for ten dollars an hour.

The police headquarter resembled of a huge open-plan office with a labyrinth of partitions and corridors. After the cops took off our handcuffs, we had to sit down in a corner at a table. The cops offered cigarettes and coffee. We were questioned and interrogated. Of course, the cops found out that our tourist visas had expired long time ago, that we were working illegally and, that we did not have a motorcycle license. In addition, the possession and cultivation of marijuana.

"There's a lot coming together", the cops said in the end.

Shyly I asked how much the penalty would be.

"You probably both have to go to jail", the cops replied dryly.

George turned pale as a cheese, my stomach almost turned over. In my mind, I already saw myself sitting in one of those brutal, hierarchical American prisons, together with murderers, felons and street gang members. I knew that I had no chance there as a sheltered youngster from Switzerland - my life was broken and botched, I was only twenty-one years old... I didn't even dare to think about my parents...

The officials confiscated our passports, declared that we would receive a court summons in the next few days, then they let us go. Dejected and depressed we took the bus home. There we thought about to escape away illegally, across the green border to Mexico or Canada. However, we rejected this idea as too risky and too dangerous and decided to wait for the court summons first. The next day we went to work as normal as if nothing had happened. After two weeks we received the court summons by mail, which was already set for three days later.

We arrived at the California State Court at nine o'clock in the morning, right on time. Carefully, George knocked on the courtroom door. After a while a uniformed security man opened the door. We were quite astonished; with their backs turned to us, about a hundred people sat on long wooden benches, all men. At the front of the hall was a raised desk, at which a judge and two other men sat, all three in gleaming black official attire. The uniformed man, after seeing our court summons, referred us to two empty seats in the back row of the benches.

It took quite some time until we had checked, that all this many people were not spectators rather all accused like us. Apparently, there was an appeal in progress. The judge had already reached the letter F in the Alphabet, so it couldn't take long before it was my turn. And right...after four or five more names, the judge's voice called out: Glas Eno...I testified my presence by standing up briefly and saying...yes.

After the appeal, the actual trial began. Each accused was called up again, had to move forward and stop there on a floor mark, three yards in front of the judge's desk. A court case lasted about five minutes each. The twelve, thirteen defendants who came before me were charged with relatively minor offences such as trespasssing, drug use, drunk driving. Some Mexicans were expelled from the country for illegal residence and undeclared work. This meant, that immediately after the trial they were deported back to the Mexican border in buses. George and I looked at each other anxiously. Then I was the first of the two of us.

"Glas Eno, please step forward", called the judge.

As if in trance I got up, stepped with soft knees to the judge's desk. On the marking line, three yards in front of it, I stopped. The judge looked at me briefly, after a look at the files he raised his voice...

"Mr. Eno Glas, citizen of Switzerland, you are accused of possession and cultivation of marijuana, illegal residence and illegal work in this country. You are also illegally driving a 500 cubic Honda without a driving-license. Do you plead to these crimes guilty or not guilty?", the judge asked.

My knowledge of English was limited at that time, the judge spoke very fast official English - I understood only more or less half. What the hell *guilty* did mean? I had no idea, what should I answer now? So, I said, just to say something, in fairly broad Swiss English: "It's the first time in my life, I was smoking marijuana."

The judge looked at me with big eyes and crooked mouth. Behind my back, the other defendants laughed and shouted, some whistled, some even bawled. I felt the sweat dripping from my armpits, my face turned red... I would have loved to hide in a mouse-hole! That was probably the dumbest answer I could give. The judge tapped at the desk with the hammer and ordered silence - I was feeling just embarrassed!

"Do you understand English or do you need a translator?" he asked me. "I understand English, I don't need a translator", I replied clumsy.

"Okay", said the judge, "will you *plead guilty* or not *guilty*?" Oh shit, that *guilty* again, what was the meaning of this? Of course, I didn't know what *plead* means, to *plead*, it sounded like *play* to me. What could I say? I blacked out completely!

Behind my back the other defendants whispered silently: "Say guilty, say guilty, say guilty"...So, I just said guilty, without knowing what it means...The judge seemed satisfied with this answer. He asked me what would happen to an American with the same offences in Switzerland. I understood what he meant and replied: "I think he will get deported."

The judge grinned wide, and replied triumphantly: *"What a great place we are! In this country you will only get a penalty of one hundred Dollars. God bless America! I recommend you not to leave the US for the next 10 years, because you could have trouble by departure!"*

The judge hit the table three times with the hammer, declared my case closed. At the end he handed me a certification, on which he had put his signature and a stamp, telling me to report to the *Room 101*...the other defendants applauded and cheered - I did not understand the world any more...I left the courtroom quite confused. I waited for George in the gangway. After half an hour he came as well. "Eno, you're a crazy number", he said with a laugh, "completely off your feet, you're lucky they didn't arrest you for stupidity."

"What the fuck means *guilty* and not *guilty?*", I asked him desperately.

"*Guilty or not guilty*...means in German: *Schuldig oder nicht schuldig,*" said my friend, patting me on the shoulder. "If you had pleaded innocent, the trial would have continued. You would have had to prove your innocence, with a lawyer, that would have been a long time turn and expensive..."

"Why didn't you tell me about this in advance, if you know everything so well?'

"Unfortunately, I didn't check on the procedure until after your trial. When you were standing there in front of the judge, I sweated blood and prayed for you, and I haven't prayed for a damn long time! In spite of everything we were lucky, even I have to pay only a hundred dollar fine."

We had to interrupt our conversation for a moment and step aside, because a black guy skated past us in the corridor of the courthouse. When he saw me, he grinned and shouted: "Cool man, you are so kiddy!"

I did not feel cool at all, smiled back embarrassed and thought...Shit man!

"By the way, Eno, did you know that in George Orwell's novel »1984«, *Room 101* is the torture chamber, called the *Ministry of Love.*"

"I didn't know that, I don't give a shit. I hope they torture you first."

After we found *Room 101*, we knocked on the door. "Come in", called a friendly female voice.

"The Ministry of Love", mumbled George, "Okay, I'll go first"... I whispered back.

With a suppressed grin but serious faces we entered a small office where a uniformed woman stood behind a counter. She demanded our certification papers, said we had to pay a hundred dollars penalty each – a snip! We paid cash over the counter, the woman gave us a receipt and - oh wonder, in addition also our Swiss passports. She declared the matter as closed.

We couldn't believe it…for so many crimes we were punished just a hundred dollars - no jail, no country reference, no nothing. That meant that we were still allowed to live illegal in the US, work, ride motorcycles and smoke pot - that was really generous of the Ame-rican justice system. Until this day I still do not understand why we got off so lightly back then.

A few months later, when leaving the country at the airport custom, I had an anxious moment - my tourist visa had expired months ago. Since the judge had practically said that I was not allowed to leave the country for ten years, I was prepared for the worst. But no custom officer wanted to see my passport, fortunately there was no exit control at all - it took a heavy load off my mind."

The Swami could only shake his head.

"Your American stories are really great, real unique, you should make a book out of them."

"It would probably be banned in America, Swami, and a bestseller in the rest of the world."

"I can tell you why you got off so lightly", he said, "For the Yanks, you were young, well trained fresh meat from Europe - they wanted to keep you. You both earned well, you both worked as specialists in large corporations, and they didn't want to let you leave. I think your employers had a big influence in this!"

"You're probably right, Swami, it must have gone that way, there's no other explanation!"

One morning I drove with a rickshaw to Pondicherry, taking advantage of the coolness early in the morning. I had set in my mind to finally acquire a small *Ganesh* statue, which I had been wishing for a long time. If possible, made of red clay, about the size as a fist.

After a breakfast at the *Hot Breads,* I visited all the souvenir shops, god shops and boutiques of Pondi. I did not find anything. Despite a long search I could not find a *Ganesh* statue that suited me. Either they were too big, too clumsy, without contours or made of metal - I probably had somewhat too concrete ideas. My last hope was a market on the beach. In a huge tent all the gods and statues of saints from India were offered there. But even there I could not find anything. There were indeed *Ganeshas* of red clay, but they looked more like a piggy bank than an elephant. There was actually a slit on the back where you could throw money in - I had never seen that before, a piggy bank *Ganesh*!

At four in the afternoon I still had not found my *Ganesh*. I was tired, my feet hurt, a little frustrated and resigned, I decided to give up the search, go back home.

Just as I was looking for a rickshaw, waving my hand, I saw - I couldn't believe my eyes - at the side of the road, in the gutter, in the dirt...a small *Ganesh* statue made of red clay, exactly as I had imagined it. I bent down, lifted the little *Ganesha* out of the gutter, thought - If the Indians start throwing away their gods now, this country will soon go down the hill!

Some Indians looked astonished - a Westerner digging in the dirt in the gutter?!

"You are my *Ganesha*", I said half-loud, "you are the one I have been looking for all day long!"

With a handkerchief I cleaned the *Ganesh* a little. He was slightly damaged, one hand was broken off. "You may have a small handicap, but I don't mind, you will get a nice place over the fireplace at home, on my Indian altar, together with your parents *Parvati* and *Shiva.*"

Little *Ganesh* was happy and grateful that I had rescued him from the gutter and had not thrown him back there immediately because of his handicap.

The Swami was visibly touched and impressed when I showed him the *Ganesh* in the evening and told him the story of how we had found each other.

"The Indian gods seem to like you very much! This is exactly the material from which the magic of coincidence synchronicity is woven."

"Eno, what do you think about fasting with me for ten days and keeping silent, not talking during this time?", the Swami asked me one morning as we were sitting at breakfast.

"Wow, ten days of fasting and silence?! Well, I don't know...three days I might last, but ten long days?! Hm...there is not much weight on me anyway, according to my body mass index I am twenty pounds underweighted. I should be on a diet to fatten up. The silence is less frightening, but fasting for such a long time gets to my substance, look at me, Swami, I am only skin and bones anyway."

"Oh, Eno, ten days fasting is nothing at all, I have fasted above in the Himalayas forty days and I am still alive! We're both so thin, we can't even lose weight, don't worry about your weight."

"Well, I'll have to think it over carefully. If so, then I want to be one hundred percent there and not just half-heartedly saying yes."

"That's a good attitude, Eno, important decisions should be considered, weighed and thought through! I don't want to persuade or push you into anything, so I don't want to give a long lecture on fasting right now. It's your choice! If you say no, that's okay too, I won't look at you as a weakling. You don't have to prove anything to me. Those are weaklings who do something to please others, who have no opinion of their own, who are not themselves."

"One more thing I would like to know, Swami, why are we silent during the time of fasting?"

"That we may better hear the Great Spirit!"

"Sounds plausible and logical...you know what, I'm going to take a little morning walk on the beach, take a dip in the ocean, let the whole thing slip around my mind."

Actually, I already knew the answer, but first I wanted to be sure what I was getting into, what it meant...

I walked a little along the beach, took a long bath, sat down on the shore for a while, pondered back and forth, let the sand trickle from one hand to the other, watched a ship in the distance...After a while I went back to our tree.

"Swami, I've decided, I'm in - when do we start?"

"Eno, I'm glad to hear that! I knew you'd say yes. So, I wasn't wrong about you. You will not regret your decision. We get a special herbal syrup enriched with minerals from the Ayurveda shop. We then take two tablespoons of this syrup every day. We would also need salt, there is almost none left." "No problem, Swami, I'll go into town tomorrow, get us the stuff."

The next morning, I took the bus again to Pondi. Of course, I decided to eat really good and well before the fasting, because finally, there was nothing to bite for ten days afterwards!

At first, I enjoyed a cappuccino and two croissants at the *Hot Breads* bakery. After that I went to the Ayurveda shop, where I bought a bottle of the aforementioned syrup and a can of sea salt.

At the GPO I met Brian, a buddy I knew from Varanasi, where we had taken a bath together in the Ganges, the holy river of the Hindus - I decided to open the letter I had received from Erica under our tree later on.

Brian was forty-five years old, English. Among other places he had lived with shamans in Mexico, spent two years as a disciple of an Indian Swami, and also spent a long time in a Buddhist monastery. His main interest, however, were hallucinogenic, psychedelic substances such as Ayahuasca, Psilocybin or Mescaline.

Brian and I went to the *Aristo* Restaurant for lunch. While Brian ordered a relatively modest meal and a soda to drink, I ordered three courses, the finest of the finest, with two bottles of Kingfisher beer.

"Hey, Eno, what happened to you?" Brian wondered. "Did you go among the gourmets, did you win the lottery, is it your birthday?"

I told him about the Swami, the tree, what I had experienced there and that from tomorrow on we would fast and keep silent for ten days.

"Wow, man, that's a hell of a story." Brian marveled, "I can understand why you're treating yourself to something special today. I fasted in a Buddhist monastery for forty days - I gained insights, knowledges and consciousness that I would never have recognized in this way, and this has shaped and changed my life forever!"

After dinner we exchanged travel stories, experiences, adventures and insights, over Coffee, *Lassis* and Indian nut tarts - Brian really had something up in his sleeve, he combined and analyzed things in a similar way as the Swami.

It was late afternoon when we took farewell. Because the buses were hopelessly congested at this time of day, the people were even standing on the running boards, I took a rickshaw back to our village.

There I met the Swami, who was sitting at Amukaram's, eating a huge portion of fish curry with rice.

"Hello, Swami, dude, looks like this is your last meal – the executioner's last meal so to speak!" I joked.

"Hello, Eno, you look like you got some goodies stuffed inside to you too?"

"Indeed! I have feasted and boozed like a king. And above, I ran into an old buddy. We spent the whole afternoon gabbing in the *Aristo*."

"I am glad to hear, Eno, that you've had a good time. Tomorrow is the end of eating, drinking and yakking, from tomorrow on asceticism is the order of the day!"said the Swami in a joking tone."

Under the tree I finally opened Erica's letter:

> Dear Eno,
>
> How are you doing? I hope you are safe and doing well. Unfortunately, I have some very sad news for you. Your friend, our friend Angelo took his own life yesterday! He threw himself off a cliff in the *Verena* Canyon! Everyone is shocked and sad! I'm just crying! I wanted to tell you a lot of things, but I am paralyzed, I can't write at the moment!
>
> Dear Eno, I hope to see you again in spring - I miss you very much, especially now!
>
>   In infinite love
>   Erica

Erica's dried-up tears on the letter mingled with mine on the paper. I sat there like a stone!

After a while I handed the letter to the Swami without a word. His tears mingled with Erica's and mine.

That was a hard blow! - So suddenly out of nowhere! What happened was so close, but because of the spatial distance it was so far away.

The Swami and I spent a quiet, reflective evening.

"Eno, we can also postpone the fast if you want and start on another day."

"It's all right, Swami, we'll start tomorrow - now more than ever!"

Before going to bed we played a game of chess. Afterwards we held a meditation to get in the mood for what was to come.

"Is there anything or something, Eno, you'd like to ask me or tell me? You know, from tomorrow on, we'll be silent for ten days."

"Hm...I want to thank the Great Spirit for leading me under this tree - to the Tree of Knowledge! I also want to thank you, Swami, for having the patience to teach me, for accepting me as your student and friend. It means a lot to me to be here with you, infinitely much - it is a gift!"

"Bum Shiva!" said the Swami and remained silent for a moment.

"I, too, have one or two things to tell you...

First about fasting: In order to prevent hunger from eating up our organs and tissues, we should take a lot of exercise - walks on the beach, swimming, Yoga. It would be wrong to just hang around lazily to save calories.

I also thank to the Great Spirit for leading you to me under the Tree of Knowledge. Thank you, Eno, for giving me your trust. I like you very much, I enjoy every day with you, you have become like a son to me - Bum Shiva! I would like to ask you, to tell me one more of your *America stories* on the last evening before the big silence.

"No problem, dude, if this is your last wish... It's fine for me.

Well, once I was sitting late at night in Atlanta Downtown, a dangerous area, in a pretty seedy Burger King restaurant. After a while, one of those tattooed Harley Rocker guys with long, greasy hair and broad shoulders sat down at my table for two. I knew instinctively...here comes trouble!

"I like your shirt," the guy said.

That day I wore a T-shirt which showed a toilet bowl and the headline: *Let's get the shit together!*

"Thanks for the compliment, I like it too."

"I want your T-shirt," said the guy with scowl eyes.

"I can't just take my shirt off in here right now", I considered.

"I'll wait for you outside", the rocker replied. From my dialect he concluded that I probably wasn't from around here and asked me, "Where are you from?" Because Switzerland embodies the reputation of wealth and money, I said, "from Finland."

The Rocker looked incredulous: "Are you kidding me? There is no such country!"

It looked like the guy was confusing Fin land with End land, and there really was no such country.

"Yes, yes...Finland, it is in Europe, Scandinavia", I replied.

The Rocker whispered with a grim look, "You fucking son of a bitch - Transylvania doesn't exist either, I'll break all your bones outside, you motherfucker! - The Rocker had obviously misheard, or mixed something up with Dracula. It had been clear to me for a long time that the Americans had no idea about global geography, but I hadn't thought that I would get into so much trouble because of it.

Slowly I had the shit no longer together, but in my pants... the rocker stood up and went outside.

Through the window front I could watch him gesticulating wildly outside, talking to half a dozen similar looking rockers. The whole gang was now looking threateningly through the window front to me...I felt really queasy - I had already eaten my burger, drank the shake - I couldn't sit here forever!

How do I get out of here... Suddenly I saw a glimmer of hope, I got up and went to the back, to the cash desk and whispered quietly to a saleswoman, "I have a problem", pointing discreetly to the window front. The saleswoman immediately understood the situation and just as discreetly opened the back entrance of the Burger King for me. To the rockers, it looked like I was going to the bathroom. I thanked the pretty Afro saleswoman, slipped through the back door, ran down the street for two blocks and arrived undisturbed via a detour at my hotel.

In the morning, when I pulled up the curtains to have a look outside, I jumped in shock, right away a step backwards - in the bar opposite, which was seated outside, sat this rocker guy with half a dozen of his cronies. It was obvious that they were watching the hotel entrance and had their eyes on the windows – luckily, I went unnoticed!

How did they find out where I live? I asked myself. Probably the rocker bride, who was sitting at the table, had simply asked at the hotel reception, whether a young blond guy, wearing a T-shirt with an illustrated toilet bowl, lived here. Perhaps they had asked the numerous prostitutes standing around, whom I had passed on my way back from the Burger King. My hasty walk and the toilet bowl were surely also noticed by them.

"Oh shit", I thought, "the day is off to a good start! How do I get out of this hotel unnoticed?"

Through the curtain gap I watched the rockers, it felt like being in the Wild West - only a *Winchester* was missing! It was ten in the morning, eleven o'clock, my Greyhound bus was leaving for Houston, Texas. The seat was booked and paid. I had to leave in the next quarter of an hour - good advice was expensive!

In the next room I heard the cleaning lady vacuuming. I asked her if the hotel had a back exit. She denied and said there is only the exit fire escape. Unfortunately, not behind the house, but well visible for the Rockers, on the left side of the building. Feverishly I pondered, peering out of the curtain gap...suddenly I saw my chance in the form of a yellow school bus, which slowly drove up the street at walking pace in the morning rush hour. I put on my rucksack, ran down the hotel stairs, called the receptionist, "Good bye, I'm too late" - luckily, I had paid the day before. When the school bus was right between the hotel entrance and the bar, I stepped out onto the street using the big bus as a cover and just walked along with it at its side. At the next cross road I turned left. As fast as my legs carried me, I ran to the nearby Greyhound station. There the bus to Houston was already waiting, the passengers slowly filled the seats. I bought myself a coffee with two donuts, got on the bus and sat down on my reserved seat. Ten minutes later the bus left - it took a load off my heart!

And, believe it or not, Swami, there was a beautiful young Indian woman sitting on the next seat. - I had never been to India before, she was the first Indian person I met. The young woman had just immigrated to the USA from India and wanted to visit relatives in Houston. We talked animatedly during the whole trip. I told her about Switzerland, she told me about India. For her, in turn, I was the first Western person she had ever spoken to. - It's crazy, there's millions of Westerners, and I was the first one? I was very honored and blessed...

During a stopover, when the Indian woman was in the refreshment room...an old American woman, who was sitting one row of seats behind us, said to me in a nagging tone, "Watch out, these Mexicans steal like magpies! "I was slowly getting angry of the

American understanding of the rest of the world, and I answered, "Listen, you old rag...this isn't a Mexican, this is an Indian!"

The old American didn't let herself be impressed: "She lies, in reality she is a Mexican", she claimed.

"And you, what are you? You also lie, because in reality you are not American, you are from Russia" I countered. I was terribly upset inside, I would have loved to grab this old, brainwashed aunt by the throat!"

The Swami, laughed and bawled, "Eno I love your *American stories.* That was a cool story before the big silence!

The next morning, after waking up, we first practiced Yoga for half an hour, followed by a meditation of about the same length. Since I did a few yoga exercises every morning, I had become much more flexible and agile. My previously bad posture had improved considerably. Instead of my beloved *Idlis* with Chutney, this morning there was only a tablespoon full of syrup. Hunger, however, was not yet a major issue. But the silence - until now rather dismissed as trivial - caused me some trouble. It didn't seem so easy after all! My need to communicate was greater than I had assumed.

How, I wondered, should I go around this day without any conversation? This promised to be quite boring and dull...Somehow time passed. In the evening a slight hunger came up.

After we had not done much on the first day, we silently cleaned our tree home on the second day, washed all our clothes, took a bath in the sea. I spent the afternoon reading the Sri Aurobindo biography. In the evening the hunger gnawed considerably. I dreamed of a fish curry.

On the third day, after the morning meditation, I fell into a depression, a feeling of senselessness. I thought, -What the fuck? That's not the point! Why, for whom and why should I chasten myself like this? I was about to call the whole thing off. Let the old man think what he likes about me! What do I care!

The Swami seemed to read my mind. He put his arm around my shoulder, looked me in the eyes for a moment. Then we went down to the beach where we took a long walk. Afterwards I felt much better, I was glad that I had held out, not given up. In the afternoon I read the rest of the Sri Aurobindo biography. The life path, the thoughts, the philosophy of this freedom fighter and guru impressed me very much.

In the morning of the fourth day I felt super good, no trace of hunger anymore. My thoughts were crystal clear. The colors of my surrounding seemed more intense than before. The green of our tree shone even greener, the blue of the sea shone even bluer. The salty sea air also smelled more intense. Despite the Indian heat, I shivered slightly. Towards evening, when it was not so hot anymore, we jogged along the beach. I was astonished how much condition I still had despite food withdrawal. In the night I dreamed again an abstract confusion that can hardly be described with words.

On the fifth day I felt all the colors and smells even more intense. I also felt the sounds, the distant waves of the surf, the chirping of the birds, the buzzing of the bees louder, more clearly than usual. I thought the Swami looked different too. I noticed features of him that I had not noticed before. At times he seemed very cunning and funny. When I looked at him, I just had to laugh.

On the sixth day I felt for a moment an intense longing and desire for a woman. I wished Erica would be here... I wonder if the Swami was thinking about Lisa. I actually found that our thoughts were often very similar or even the same. Sometimes I had the impression that we communicated together even though we didn't speak at all, a kind of telepathy. Strange...I wondered if he felt the same way.

In the morning of the seventh day, it seemed to me as if I had hardly slept because of so many dreams. Often the dreams were about my past. I realized that I had probably made some mistakes in my life, missed some opportunities, and had kept up some relationships with girl-friends for too long.

After seven days of fasting I still felt amazingly fit physically. I wasn't even thinking about food anymore. It seemed rather strange to eat at all. It seemed strange to me that we spent so much time around food - shopping, cooking, eating, washing up, cleaning up - without food we would have three hours more every day to disposal. I also saw that I often, especially in Europe, ate the wrong food - too few vegetables and fruits, too much sugar, too much fast food!

While jogging in the evening I flew light as a feather over the beach. The following game of chess I played concentrated as never before. The Swami still won, but I stayed a lot longer, saw possibilities and combinations that I had not noticed or thought of before.

In the morning of the eighth day, when I opened my eyes after meditation, I felt that our tree was alive, had a soul, it seemed to move very easily, the branches appeared to me like long tentacles. The tree sap that dripped at one point was the blood of the tree...I realized, that trees are not stiff and dead... they need some wind and they move and in a strong wind they even dance.

The Swami seemed to me like a goblin from another time and world.

On the ninth day of fasting and silence my whole perception, my whole senses were heightened in every way. I finally realized that I had not landed under that tree by chance. These apparent concatenations of coincidence were precisely timed events. The appa-rent chaos possessed an order!

On the tenth morning of fasting I woke up early. It took at least two hours until sunrise...The Swami sat on his mat, lit by two candles, meditating. Some incense sticks emitted a pleasant fragrance. When he noticed that I had woken up, he waved me over to him, pointing to me to take a seat opposite him.

For a long time, we sat in silence. I knew he was up to something... After a while he took out a metal box from his bag, which contained a green-brown powder. He stirred three heaped spoons of this powder into our cups and mixed it with water.

Slowly, in small sips we sipped the bitter-sour tasting drink that the Swami had prepared from the herbal powder...

I closed my eyes, slight dizziness seized me, I had to lie down. In the far distance I heard an *Om* chanting that carried me into an orange light. After a while I opened my eyes, the orange light remained, did not disappear. As much as I tried to see something, I only saw an orange light. A panic seized me, I was afraid to go blind, to see the rest of my life only orange. After a while I started to accept the orange - actually it was a beautiful color. I realized that it was my own inner fire, at the same time it was the fire of the whole universe.

Slowly the orange light gave way to a violet shimmer and finally dissipated. I could see normally again. A deep gratitude seized me that I had been allowed to experience this fire.

The Swami sat motionless, frozen to a Shiva statue, with eyes closed, in the lotus seat on his raffia mat. A wave of affection and love flooded through me. I was infinitely happy that I was allowed to be with him, that he was at all hanging out with me, that I was allowed to be his friend.

A black crow now sat down on a branch of our tree, somehow it seemed very depressed and sad. After a while I saw Angelo, my deceased friend, in the crow.

"Eno", he said, "forgive me, I screwed up, I committed a huge stupidity. I gave up and threw away my precious, valuable life for nothing. I have put a black shadow around the soul of my parents, relatives and friends. I did deeply wrong. Eno, you were my best friend, together we travelled India, experienced many adventures and had endless conversations. You were the most profound, imaginative and creative person I have ever met in my life. Eno, you will not have an easy life, you will have to endure and suffer several blows of fate and several injustices. Even if life sometimes seems hopeless and desperate - you should not choose my way out, it is a dead end! I will soon have to reincarnate again, get a new body, start all over again - and it won't get any easier. Eno, my friend, hold on, go until the end, straight, proud and with brave like a warrior! We will meet again!"

At these words the crow jumped off the branch and fluttered away.

Again, I became dizzy, an undertow seized me and carried me to a holiday camp, to an eight-room with seven comrades, where I spent three weeks as a ten-year-old.

One evening before the lights went out, we were all sitting on our beds, I entertained my comrades with self-made improvised jokes and comic stories, in imitated English, Russian or Low German. I faxed and jerked around like a clown. An old stinky sock served me as a requisite and I always came up with new stories and jokes. My comrades bent over with laughter!

Suddenly the door of our room slammed open, the lock and the hinges trembled! The teacher Marti, a tall, corpulent, grey-haired man, rushed straight at me with a bright red head. He literally beat me up with his huge paws, which were more suited to a construction worker, all blows to the head.

"Get up, come with me!!!" he yelled. When I wanted to put on my slippers, he shouted: "Without slippers!" And he slapped me again, so much that it was just clapping. Now he dragged me outside the door into the hallway. With a chalk he drew a cross on the floor by the right door post. "You stay here until I come back", he commanded in a threatening tone. "Don't you move!"

So, there I stood, a little boy of ten years, completely intimidated and demolished, barefoot in pyjama on the cold stone floor. In the corridor a weak night lamp was burning, on the wall a big clock was ticking, which showed nine. The hours passed slowly...I heard every second. The whole house was silent and quiet, only the big clock was ticking. Forty children slept in their beds. I was the only one outside the door. Never before had I felt so lonely and abandoned, so powerless and sad - after all, I was a child in a holiday camp, the first time away from home without parents!

At four o'clock in the morning, after seven hours, the teacher's wife showed compassion to me and let me back into the bedroom. When it was time to get up, I felt miserable, battered and sick. I got a summer flu, had a fever and had to stay in bed for a few days.

I sat up...tears were streaming down my cheeks...I realized in that night: the comedian, the clown, the entertainer inside me died! He was literally beaten out, then punished, the illness gave him the rest - never again after that I could play the clown, the comedian, often I envied others when they cut faces or grimaces, and telling jokes – I was blocked! - suffered from it, even though I was once a master clown! Later I tried to cover this shortcoming, this deficit with coolness - but you don't make friends with cold! I was lonely - once a gifted entertainer.

I realized how much this teacher Marti had destroyed in me. I grasped the full implications, the full tragedy. This teacher had hundreds of children on his conscience, hundreds spent two long years in his class under his wings. How many ran a lifetime around as psycho cripples because of this tyrant? - After all, I was lucky, I had only to spend three weeks together with him in a vacation camp!

"Teacher Marti, you bastard, you child beater, I hate you till the end of my days, I'll shoot you, stab you, hang you up, you shall burn in hell forever!"

"Eno", said a voice admonishing without anyone speaking, "now it's enough, it's enough...you won't get anywhere with hatred, it won't make you free! You must forgive the teacher Marti with all your heart. Forgiveness takes place in the heart!"

How could I ever forgive that devil, this monster? - He had caused too much suffering to me and others.

"You must try to forgive him, it's the only chance", the voice warned me, "the only way to free yourself from this trauma, this blockade, otherwise this teacher Marti will hang on you like a limpet for the rest of your life. With hate you destroy only yourself - then the teacher Marti has finally won! You don't have to love him. You just have to forgive him."

The voice was right, it spoke the truth. What it said seemed perfectly logical. I sat in meditation posture, visualized the teacher Marti, took a deep breath and concentrated on my heart.

"Teacher Marti", I said, "you have done me a great damage, a big injury! I have suffered greatly from this. Someone destroyed your own clown too...that's why you couldn't stand kids which still had their clown in them. They reminded you of your own broken clown, of your own suffering. You weren't allowed to be a clown, so the others couldn't be either! How many kids have you beaten the clown out? There is no reason to hate you, you too carry your Karma and you will be held accountable on the deathbed! I sincerely forgive you for what you did."

Warmth flooded through me, inner peace spread, my heart opened...the teacher Marti slowly crumbled to dust, like Count Dracula at the end of the film - I took a breath, I was free!

I got up, fetched my shaving mirror, looked in, stuck out my tongue, rolled my eyes, wrinkled my nose, grimaced, laughed and bellowed - finally, after eighteen years I had found my clown again! I thanked the Great Spirit for this gift. The clown was happy too, he cried with joy that he too had found me again after so long.

Lying on my mat, I looked at the crown of our tree. It seemed more beautiful than ever before. It revealed to me all its splendor, all its grace, its whole being. I saw patterns, ornaments, mandalas, colors that I had never realized and seen before on it. The crown of the tree turned into a green spiral, a green vortex that was spinning faster and faster, pulling me into its center with its suction. The center was a green tunnel. My heart was pounding, I got scared. What awaited me at the end of this tunnel? - Was the end waiting there, was death waiting there? I shook my head. I didn't want to go into this tunnel. I turned away from the tree top. But I was irresistibly attracted to it. The green spiral began to turn again...again I turned away - No, I didn't want to - why should I, what was the point of that...?

From far away I heard the voice say: "Eno, don't be so afraid, the whole thing is just a game. Try it again."

A feeling of cowardly failure came over me. This cowardly feeling became so strong, that I could hardly stand it any longer...again the spiral began to turn, the tunnel center threatened to pull me inside. I felt at the other end of the tunnel, on the other side, something wonderful was waiting for me, what could it be? I felt an incredible fear of this uncertainty - No, I did not want to go through this tunnel, which now seemed like a birth canal to me. I'd rather be a coward for the rest of my life than going through that tunnel! The pressure of the coward, the bad feeling of failure, however, became stronger and stronger, threatening to crush me. At the end it was bigger than my fear of the tunnel - it was unbearable! I had to surrender to the spiral, had to go through the tunnel, whatever was waiting for me on the other side!

I took a deep breath, relaxed...slowly surrendered to the ever faster spinning spiral. The center was getting closer and closer... My curiosity about the other side was now greater than my fear. Now the undertow pulled and tore me with all its might into the tunnel - there was no escape!

White light shone, my whole body, every single cell, trembled, vibrated and shivered. Supernovas in all rainbow colors exploded in my head - an orgasmic feeling of happiness flooded through me! The tree was also shaking and quivering. Together we merged, we became all-one. It gave me all his strength and love, I in turn gave it all my love and strength.

Exhausted, I slowly released myself from the tree, thanking it with all my heart for his gift. All trees, flowers, bushes and grasses applauded, congratulated me for my performance and gave me standing ovations. Gratefully, in all humility, I accepted their homage.

I sat down outside in front of our tree to a reddish granite stone the size of a beer crate. Until now I did not pay much attention to this stone, it just laid there. Now I noticed that he was the only one far and wide. The soil here was sandy, underneath was red clay. Large stones were rare in this area. How could this stone have gotten here, to this place?

For a while I looked at him... Suddenly this *dead* stone began to deform slightly. It was like a breathing, it contracted a little and expanded back into the original form. It reminded me of a sponge with very small capillaries, it was not just dead, rigid and lifeless - it was alive! It couldn't be... I closed my eyes. I could accept that plants had a life, but stones - never! Rocks are dead!

As if under compulsion I opened my eyes, I couldn't help it, I just had to look at it...again the stone began to breathe, to live, wanted to draw me under its spell. Startled, I closed my eyes again. I was totally afraid to become a stone myself - a stone for all eternity?

"Why, you're so afraid, Eno, why are you so cowardly? This is only a stone", said the distant voice, "just go into this stone, completely relaxed." Again, I looked at the stone - no, I could not enter the stone, never ever!

"Bullshit – what's this all about? Leave me alone with this stupid stone!"

"Eno, you cover your fear, your incapacity, your cowardice with defiance", replied the distant voice, "you are a cowardly defiant head."

"I do not care, I give a shit, if I'm cowardly and defiant who cares, I don't give a damn!" but I felt more and more rotten, worse and uncomfortable with that cowardly defiant head...

"Okay, okay, I'll just go into this rock..."

I looked at it disgruntled and grumpy, wanted to get it over and done.

"Eno, it doesn't work that way. You're still as defiant as a little boy. You must open your heart and connect with this stone with love."

Even that too - why he did not ask desire for everything! But I understood that this was the only chance to get rid of the heavy burden of the defiant head.

Again, I looked at the stone...actually it didn't look that bad - on the contrary, it was a beautiful stone! It had an aesthetic form and shape and I liked his color as well.

Slowly, I relaxed...slowly I opened up myself to it...Gently the stone pulled me inside - I surrendered myself to the stone! It showed me its full splendor, grace and beauty...why hadn't I noticed that before?

I slid deeper and deeper into the stone, merged with it, became a stone myself. Suddenly the stone gave off a sound - a billion-year-old tone of infinite depth and beauty. Then it began to tell: "We stones also live, we are not dead and lifeless, we are the oldest life of all - the primordial life. We live on the moon, on Mars, on Venus. We live in the whole universe. We are the basis of all other material life. However, we live so slowly that it is neither measurable, nor recognizable, nor understandable for you humans - yet we live! Because we live so slowly, we practically live forever. One breath takes a billion years for us. You are in a state where time is suspended, where there is no more time, where time is relative...It was very nice meeting you, it was a pleasure...It is very rare that a human being enters the stone kingdom."

Again, I was overcome by this insane, orgasmic feeling of happiness. I saw everything that the stone kingdom had to offer - glittering, sparkling crystals, emeralds, sapphires, opals, diamonds, all the wealth, all the splendor...it was overwhelming! I thanked the stone that it had initiated me into his secret, that it had revealed itself to me. It also thanked me for having given myself to it, for having listened to it.

Slowly I detached myself from the stone, went back under our tree, where I laid down on my mat. I wondered what happened next, what kind of test awaited me? Slowly I understood the course of the game, the meaning of the tests and examinations.

Again, I heard the distant voice. "Eno, do you really like animals, do you love them?"

"Yes, of course I like animals, I love animals!"

In front of me a herd of wild horses appeared, which ran through the prairie led by the leading stallion.

In the savannah, a mother lion laid under a tree with her two cubs. A couple of elephants splashed each other in a nearby water pond. Smoothly a black panther roamed through the jungle. dolphins were cavorting in the water. A proud eagle hovered majestically above it all.

My heart leapt for joy when I saw Micky, the house cat of my childhood - how often I had petted and caressed it. When it was run over by a car, I mourned for days.

From a distance, I heard a dog barking...

"How about dogs, Eno, do you love them?"

"Well, when I was a child, I was once bitten by a dog, a German shepherd called Arno. After that I was afraid of dogs for a long time. Even later, as an adult, I did not like them very much..."

After some effort and trouble, however, I managed to get the dogs into my heart, to like them."

"What about rats, spiders and snakes?", asked the voice.

They are not exactly my favorite animals...but after a few attempts I managed to love these creatures of nature, too.

I was eagerly expected one of these cathartic orgasmic flashes, but nothing happened, apparently the exam was not yet finished.

Suddenly a whole swarm of mosquitoes flew under our tree. Of course, they smelled my blood within seconds, soon all of them swarming over me. In all the weeks over here, I had not seen a single mosquito. Al-though ubiquitous in India, they avoided our tree. Either they did not like cashew nut trees or the foliage was just too dense for them - today seemed to be an extraordinary day!

"How about the mosquitoes?", asked the voice. "You said you love all animals - even mosquitoes count as animals. It is not a great art to love horses and dolphins. But it is a great art to love mosquitoes."

"Oh voice, you're fucking hard. How can a person love these stinging bloodsuckers - that is impossible!"

"Eno, nothing is impossible, try it once! Just imagine a sweet, adorable little, tiny mosquito."

I tried to relax, to open up... No, no way...I couldn't do it, impossible...

The first Mosquito sat on my thigh, I twitched my leg, it flew away...on my eyebrow. With my hand I clapped at it. Now they tried it in pairs, one on my foot, another on my forehead. I waved around me. The buzz of the swarm became unbearable. The fight with the mosquitoes took quite some time - hopeless, there were too many of them! Finally, I surrendered, gave myself to them - Sting me, suck me, drink my blood. I love all animals, including you!"

I relaxed, opened my heart...and behold, the whole swarm flew away as fast as it had come.

A spiral of light seized me, it rushed and trembled, a gigantic orgasmic feeling of happiness and light, flooded through me...I rode on a black stallion across the prairie, on the wings of an eagle I flew over mountains and valleys, jumped over wave crests with a dolphin, with a butterfly. I drank the nectar of a lotus flower. I understood the language of all animals. They congratulated me for my performance, thanked me for having acknowledged them, respected them and paid attention. I also thanked them. I felt deeply moved and honored that they showed me their true nature.

From far away I heard the voice again. "Eno, I also congratulate you, you have passed the test of the stone kingdom, the test of the plant kingdom, the test of the animal kingdom, and the test of the human kingdom. This was the first part of your exams, there are more tasks waiting for you!

Exhausted, battered, but infinitely happy I laid on my raffia mat.

When I looked up, the Swami was sitting meditating in the lotus position under our tree. Strange, I hadn't noticed his return... Maybe he had never been away? He looked at me for a long time.

"Eno, are you capable of becoming a beggar monk, a *sadhu*?", he asked me, without actually speaking. "Are you able to live in India as a beggar for the rest of your life?"

"Wow, Swami, I don't think so - impossible, that would be badass!", I replied, without really speaking. "I could hardly imagine a harder life form."

"There are millions of Indians who live this brutal way of life every day", replied the Swami.

"I know, but unlike me, they were born into this beggar life. I, on the other hand, come from the West, am educated, have relationships, friends, acquaintances, parents. I can't just let all this go to become a mendicant monk in India. I don't think this is my destiny."

Again, two voices were fighting inside me - one insisted on my arguments, the other said: coward, failure, spoiled softy... I don't know how long this inner struggle lasted, whether it lasted minutes, hours or even days, I had lost all sense of time. I felt more torn up than I've ever felt in my life. My inner tension grew into the unbearable - either a mendicant monk or a cowardly, spoiled softy...

The Swami suddenly seemed very threatening. And ominous: I didn't know anymore who he really was. Maybe his whole posturing was only a show. Maybe he wasn't a Swami or a Shaman at all, but a nasty crook, a criminal, who was only after my money all the time! Maybe he was a black magician, a hypnotist, wanted to take me to the point where I would hand over my money and passport to him and then he disappears...

I got scared! What if he suddenly took the trident, held it to my throat? In my condition, I was completely helpless. Perhaps he was a ritual murderer on top of all this, even in cahoots with the cremator! I thought I saw a forty-year-old man behind the Santa Claus beard, which had only served as a camouflage...the naked horror seized me.

I got up, went to the place where my valuables were buried and started digging the plastic box out of the sand. I opened the box, took out my passport, the return ticket, the 2000 dollars, put everything together in front of the Swami on the raffia mat...Then I saw that I got away. Running, barefoot, dressed with only one pair of shorts, without a single Rupee in my pocket, I walked along the beach.

If this is really my destiny, if the Great Spirit really wants this, I will become a beggar in India. King or beggar, we are all equal on the deathbed anyway!

It was hot, the sun burned relentlessly, I became dizzy, I staggered and reeled towards a small group of palm trees, sank into the shade on the sandy ground, closed my eyes. A spiral seized me, sucked me into its center without mercy, into a black hole!

Slowly the black gave way to a blurred image. It became clearer, sharper...I was looking at a big city full of magnificent architecture, big temples and beautiful buildings. On the horizon the city merged with the dunes of a vast desert.

I sat on a chair on a covered terrace overlooking this majestic, imposing city.

A hand gently grasped mine, a female voice said, "Akhenaten, isn't it beautiful, our new built city, in the last golden light of *Aton*? The inauguration ceremony tomorrow will be a great day for all of Egypt!

Then the city of *Aton* will be the new capital of Egypt."

"And you, fair Nefertiti, are her queen. From tomorrow on, only one God will rule over all of Egypt - *Aton*, who gives light, warmth and life! I, Akhenaton son of *Aton*, and you, Nefertiti daughter of *Aton*, will rule over the whole land from his city."

"I sincerely hope, my husband, that the disempowered priests of *Amun* will not disturb tomorrow's celebrations, that they will not commit an attack."

"Don't be afraid, don't worry. They wouldn't dare. I've reinforced the guards and customs posts. Every citizen coming into the city from outside is registered and searched. I also let the high priest *Bekanchon* know: If even one *Amun* priest disturbs the festivities, I will raze all the temples of *Amun* in the whole country to the ground!"

"Certainly, my husband, tomorrow they will leave us in peace. But what will it be like the day after tomorrow? The old priests still exert great influence and have much power. Large parts of the people still pay homage to the old gods. *Bekanchon* will do anything to maintain his power!"

"I know my loyal Queen, this jackal is capable of anything. Oh, how do I hate this cold war for power! My only consolation is that we are at peace with the Hittites and Babylonians."

"Let us not spoil the evening, my beloved - *Aton* is on our side."

"Do not worry, fairest daughter of *Aton*, it is our night and tomorrow it is our day. I want to be close to you tonight, to see you happy – let's have a cup of wine on my bed..."

Then, suddenly, the picture, the scenery, changed, as if you were switching to another channel on TV.

I found myself in a tepee...it was early morning, I had just crawled out of the buffalo skins and pushed the tarpaulin at the entrance a little to the side, outside it was snowing thick white flakes. The nightly snowstorm had blown a large snowdrift to the east side of our tepee. Today was not a day to get up early! I pulled the tarp back up, went back to our bed.

For a long sequence I looked at Elina's face... how beautiful she was, how graceful. Peacefully she slept, wrapped in buffalo skin. Quietly I crawled to her, placed my skin blanket over us.

"Good morning, Little Elk, she said teasingly, snuggling.

"Good morning, Elina, you're so cozy and warm. Outside it's a fool weather, not even the bluecoats dare to come out – I like to stay with you under the skins all day long...

"That's a good idea, Little Elk, let's have a cozy day We still have some cooked dog and corn porridge left over from yesterday - what more do we want? You know what, Little Elk? I'll make some herbal tea, while you stuff a pipe of *Kinikinik*, and then we can cuddle up real nice...

"Elina, you know that smoking is strictly forbidden for woman by the Cheyenne! If we ever get caught... But it's fine with me - I also find cuddling afterwards even more beautiful, falling asleep is like being on clouds."

"You're the greatest man alive, Little Elk! No other Cheyenne man would do that with his squaw."

Peacefully we smoked a pipe of *Kinikinik*, sipped a cup of herbal tea. After that we made love so that the buffalo skins steamed...

Suddenly... "did you hear that...strange... Elina, what could that be?...Sounds like...By the Great Spirit - The Bluecoats!

Elina go, run as fast as you can to the river, hide there on the bank, I'll follow!"

In lightning hurry, I put on my leggings, slipped into the moccasins, tore the gun with the bullet bag from the hook, stuck the knife in the belt and stormed outside.

There I saw a wild and crowded picture... women screaming, men panting, shots cracking, babies crying, frightened horses neighing...a Bluecoat, who was sitting on his horse, swung his saber over my head, he missed me by a hair's breadth. Because I hadn't loaded my rifle, I couldn't defend myself. With the rifle butt I hit the Bluecoat on his knee, I heard the kneecap crack. The horse reared up, threw the Bluecoat out of the saddle, thereby he lost its saber. I pounced on him with the butt of my rifle ahead. He drew his pistol - I was a little quicker... A putt stroke hit him on the skull. The Bluecoat collapsed, my rifle broke into two parts. I grabbed his colt, ran for the river.

A Bluecoat stabbed a woman lying on the ground with his sabre...Great Spirit! - It was Elina! She was laying covered in blood in the white snow.

"Elina, I..." an unconscious rage, a merciless hate, an unending grief overwhelmed me...

As if in a trance, I fired my colt at the Bluecoat - four shots, then the drum was empty. None of my bullets hit. I'd never fired a colt before. I tore the knife from my belt, threw myself on the Bluecoat. A shot rang out behind me, it had to be very close. I felt something at the back of my head, the ground beneath me gave way, I staggered...it turned black...

After a while I woke up over a thick leather band with Plato's texts - I must have dozed off while reading, as I often do...silent but insistent, knocking on the window tore me out of my daydreams.

Who on earth could that be? Can't a guy ever get any peace?

Disgruntled, I got up, opened the window.

"Elène, darling - you? What are you doing in the back of town?"

"Edmond, you must flee the city immediately", she gasped out of breath, "the guards of the revolution were at my house, they asked for you, they are looking for you!"

"What you don't say - what they want from me? I'm not supporting that idiot of a king. That old fool should abdicate and go to hell forever! He, the court state and the nobility have sucked the people dry like ticks, now they get the bill."

"Edmond, this is not the time to argue, the revolutionary guards and the mob are killing everyone who looks like nobility, money or Huguenots!"

"Elène, I'm neither a Huguenot nor a member of the nobility, nor am I rich."

"Don't be naive, Edmond, you are wealthy, educated, widely travelled – that's enough! There have been hundreds of deaths in the city since yesterday. The guards do not differentiate greatly, nor do they hold a justice. Every wealthy citizen is in extreme danger at the moment - everyone who wears good shoes and expensive clothes, you understand, Edmond?"

"I don't believe that, I didn't do anything!"

"Edmond, you live in your intellectual world, in your book world, but that is not the real world - the real world can neither read nor write...the world is in an uproar right now. I beg you to flee before it's too late! The guards could be here any minute."

"Elène, where the hell am I gonna run to? I can't just run out of the house and run away somewhere."

"You must flee north, towards to Chantilly. My sister lives a few miles from Chantilly. You'll be safe in the country! Here, I made a drawing sketch, for you. Her husband's name is Pierre Moulin – they'll hide you. Here, I brought you some food and some old clothes. You have to change! You're too conspicuous in your fine clothes."

"All right...ok, Elène, thank you. Here, take, some money, look after the children – I'll be back as soon as things calm down again...go home now...I love you!"

Just as I was getting ready to change my clothes, I heard loud men's voices outside, heavy boots and dogs barking. A fist was banging on my door.

"Edmond, you traitor - open up!" ordered a man's voice screaming.

With one leap I jumped out of the window, behind me the door was kicked in.

"There he runs, he escaped out of the window - pursue him, he must not escape!" shouted the commander.

I ran as fast as I could down the road, across a field towards the forest, closely followed by the uniformed guards and two dogs...No chance, it was hopeless! I was no longer the youngest, I quickly lost my breath. At the edge of the forest I was caught by the dogs, thrown to the ground, and seconds later six soldiers of the revolutionary guard surrounded me.

"Edmond Dupont!" shouted the commander. "You are a traitor, a favorite of the king. You were on the wrong side, shamelessly enriching yourself on the people. The tide has turned - now we are in charge! You will be executed on the spot for treason against the people."

"Have mercy, let justice and mercy prevail", I gasped, "I have never been on the side of the king, I am neither a Huguenot nor a member of the nobility. My money is honestly earned. I have taken it from the rich, certainly not from the poor - I have given it to them often."

"Shut up, you traitor, you have benefited from this system! The tax collector George Dorne testified against you. You, have been a guest at the Royal Court several times, you have eaten and feasted, while the people were starving - long live the revolution, down with the king and his loyals!"

Aha, there we go! George Dorne, that disgusting, envious, little, fake tax collector - I could have guessed it, that cowardly informer!

I saw that there was no point in justifying myself, defending myself. These people could not be convinced by anything or anyone. In their eyes was sheer hatred - they could hardly wait to see me dead...

I had to stand against a tree, then my feet were tied together and my hands tied behind my back. The guards loaded their muskets. A few steps in front of me they took a line - so this was to be my end...the guards put on their muskets, I fixed each one of them, looked each one in the eye.

"Do what you have to do! I'm dying right here, right now, like this. Death will come for you too one day, one way or another. Perhaps your death is far more painful than mine. Maybe you get a disease, an infirmity that gnaws at you for years, tortures you. Pain that drives you crazy. In that sense, death is merciful to me. Lord, forgive my sins, forgive my trespasses Elène, I love you and our children, may God protect you!"

The muskets cracked, I felt some hot spots on my chest. My head hit something hard...

A black and white checkered spiral began to spin, pul-ling me into the center, into a tunnel. I saw Elène, my children, the happiest moments, the most beautiful experiences of my life passed by me once again...

When I opened my eyes, I lay in a strangely bent posture, hands on my back, in front of a palm tree trunk.

What kind of crazy trip was going on here? Was it all madness, vision, hallucination? I was beginning to worry I wouldn't find my way back.

I sat up, looked into the vastness of the sea, lost myself in the infinite, wide and deep blue.

A distant voice said: "Eno, your time has finally come. Up to this point everything has been a foreplay, a preparation - now the real, the true game begins! You have to say farewell to everything for final and separate de-finitely forever from live!"

My breath hesitated, over my back it was running cold... Was that now the Death speaking?

"Yes, I am the Death," said the voice, "I am a messenger, an envoy of the Great Spirit."

"Venerable Death, why must I die so young? I'm not yet thirty years old. I like so much to find the true love and my true vocation."

"I'm sorry, Eno, I understand your desire, you will get another chance in another live. Your time here on earth is over!"

The words of the Death sounded so clear, so unambiguous, so determined - it had to be so! I had no choice but to come to terms with this reality. I was overcome by an unending sadness and resignation. So much I wanted to do. Now I should let go everything, say goodbye to everything - that was hard! Death was not really the problem, letting go life was the difficulty!

"Almighty Death, it is infinitely difficult for me, but if you think that my hour has struck, it has struck. I accept your decision, declare myself ready and willing to die."

I lay on my back, stretched all fours from me, closed my eyes...After a while I didn't think it was so bad to die. What was I doing on this broken, ailing planet? I felt that where I was going now it is much more beautiful, more peaceful, more fair, much more sublime.

"Great Spirit, I am ready - you can come for me!"

I relaxed, took a few deep breaths, waited for the take-off...

Suddenly my old friend and schoolmate Ferdinand stood before me, we had not seen each other for a long time. He had grown a little older, but essentially, he looked almost the same as he did then. Ferdi was one of the funniest, humorous friends I had ever known, a real teaser. He didn't need to do much at all, the outward appearance alone was enough. The hooked nose between the owl's eyes, the lanky, asynchronous body movements, the impossible combinations of clothes caused most people to laugh. So, this Ferdi stood in front of me...

"Hello, Eno, dude, what are you doing here? You are looking very serious and sad. - What? You want to die?! Give me a break, life is much too beautiful, above all you are still much too young! Come on, get up, let's go to the nearest beach bar and have a cold beer.

Hey, Eno, do you know the difference between a snake and a car snake?"

"Hm... I don't know, Ferdi, I would think the snake is made of meat, the car snake is made of tin."

"Wrong, Eno, it's like this... a snake has the asshole at the back, a car snake has it in the front..." We both had to laugh heartily.

"That was a funny joke! Ferdi, it was nice to see you again and laugh with you. I'm afraid I can't come with you, my path is another."

At these words Ferdi dissolved, he disappeared as quickly as he had come. - This had probably been a test of whether I was really serious about dying. Again, I waited for the take-off, tried to relax, tried to beam myself away.

Someone gently grabbed my hand... I turned my head to the side.

"Elina, Elène, Erica, you...? What are you doing here?"

"I'll go with you, I'll accompany you!"

"But you can't just come with me, I'm dying here..."

"Shh...Eno, don't talk, just look me in the eyes."

Our eyes met, Erica's pupils, became a rainbow spiral, which slowly pulled me towards the center, into the iris. It shook, vibrated slightly, as if an airplane, a shuttle was taking off.

After a while we found ourselves in space, looking at our blue earth - how infinitely beautiful it was, how fragile, how precious! On closer inspection we realized how ill this wonderful earth was, unfortunately, infected by a greedy virus that destroyed and poisoned everything. - This dangerous virus was mankind! Humanity as such was greedy, false, lying, deceitful, mean, ignorant, stupid, broken and sick! - That kind of mankind was not my mankind! I felt as if I had accidentally landed on the wrong planet, I was completely happy and glad to be able to leave this backward, primitive planet. I did not shed a tear for this swamp of intrigue, lies, hatred and resentment. May the apocalypse come, may this earth sink like Sodom and Gomorrah in a ball of fire. - It would give me great satisfaction! - Just don't look back regretfully and wistfully - otherwise you might be frozen like Lot's wife to a stone pillar...

Further and further I moved away from the earth, it became smaller and smaller, until it finally dissolved into the black nothing of the universe.

When I opened my eyes, I laid on a colorful flower meadow, looking into a green valley where a turquoise river meandered. Next to me, I couldn't believe it, Erica sat... we hugged, laughing.

Around us grew beautiful flowers, exotic plants, fruits and majestic trees like we had never seen before. A colorful bird sitting in the branches of a tree, sang a magical melody like we had never heard before - truly a strange place, it looked as if we had landed in another world, on another planet. From some distance we saw a group of people moving in our direction. When they were a little closer, we could make out three women and as many men. They wore colorful, light dresses, were all tall and slender, perfect beautiful people of graceful figure and graceful movements. With open mouths we watched them. They didn't seem to have noticed us yet.

"Erica, what do you think? We could approach these people, ask them where we are."

Exactly at the moment when they actually had to see us, when we wanted to make ourselves noticed, the film tore and it went black again...

"Eno", said the distant voice, "your time is not yet ripe for you. You need to go back to your world. If these people had seen you, if you had talked to them, there would have been no going back. You get one more chance to find true love. Besides, you still have a mission to accomplish. This mission will be your vocation!"

When I opened my eyes again, the sun was almost vertical in the sky, it had to be around noon.

I was here again, alive, not dead... tears streaming down my cheeks. I thanked the Great Spirit for giving me another chance. I decided to change my life from now on and walk through the world carelessly and listen to the voice of my heart. I understood the insane gift of life, understood its meaning and significance, didn't want to waste it anymore and act more consequently.

With shaky, soft knees I rose, similar to a toddler rising for the first time. Unsteadily wavering I took the first steps in to my new life.

I felt a little clearer in my head now, grounded again to some extent. This insane trip seemed to be slowly coming to an end.

I went to the beach, sat down on the shore, let a handful of sand trickle from one hand to the other, formed a sand cake, put a decoration with some shells.

My eyes wandered to the sea...saw a few pointed fins on the surface...dolphins! An eight-headed herd romped near the shore. I watched them spellbound - what graceful, agile animals!

One of them swam very close to the shore, stuck his head out of the water and said, without actually speaking, "Hey, what are you doing crouching in the sand? Come in to the water, play with us."

As if in trance, I got up, slid into the sea, dived over the first crest of the wave and swam, escorted by the one dolphin, to the playing group.

"Don't you remember me?" he asked. "I'm the one who lost my way, the one you saved my live with your friend. That's my family over there."

"Oh, yes, I recognize you now by the little pink freckle above your eye. I didn't know you have such a big fa-mily, I thought you were more of a lone wolf."

Chattering, the whole dolphin family greeted me, they were all very excited. One after the other, every single animal swam to me, let itself be caressed, stroked, embraced. They trusted me and I trusted them!

Then we gave us into the game. I swam with them, dived with them, let myself pull through the water,

lost myself in the ecstasy of the game, dissolved, became a dolphin myself. Our game lasted a long time, again and again it started anew, did not want to end...until I slowly felt my strength dwindling.
"Hey, friends, I got to get back to the shore. I can't do it anymore. I'm tired...It was very nice together with you!"

At the same time, almost as if on command, the dolphins all dived under water. I didn't see a single fin. A moment later they all reappeared together. Eight heads looked out of the water. The dolphins had formed a circle around me. I swam in their midst, was the center. They had taken me into their midst.

Once again, the dolphins dived under all together... when they appeared, I swam with them in a circle, was part of their circle. I had been accepted into their circle. - An endless grateful feeling of happiness and luck flowed through me. I felt very honored and presented!

"I love you all, I will never forget you! You're my dolphin family forever!"

I swam back to the shore, my friend with the pink freckle accompanied me for a while - I was at the end of my force. When I felt firm ground under my feet again, my friend, slipped under my arm and swam back to his family.

Completely pumped out I laid on the beach...the feelings overwhelmed me completely...then I made my way back to our tree

When I entered the inside of the tree, the Swami sat peacefully cross-legged on his mat.

"Hello, Eno, there you are! I think we can break the silence rule now - Slowly I was getting worried about you, just wanted to have a look after you."

Very thirsty, half dry, I greedily rushed down three big cups of lime water.

"Boo...Swami, you can't imagine what I've gone through and experienced today. That was the hardest, craziest, most insightful day of my life. What the hell, what kind of a shamanic cocktail have you been giving me?"

Strangely, odd and unfamiliar sounded my voice after ten days of silence. I had to pick the words together properly, had some trouble articulating them.

"Young friend, calm down, everything is the way it always was. The whole game only happened in your head. - Come, sit down."

For a while the Swami looked into my eyes, then he said, "Eno, I know what you've been gone through, I can see it in your eyes...the drink consisted of four shamanic substances, a secret recipe from my teacher in the Himalayas.

You passed all your exams, you were great! That I did not have to intervene is the proof. Congratulations! I knew you could make it...I saw your potential on the very first day when we met! What do you think we go get something to eat? I'm hungry as a lion."

"Good idea, Swami, I hadn't thought about eating at all, but now that you mention it, it really makes my guts contract. Food, I would like to eat, although that seems to me to be rather strange. However, I have some trouble getting around people in my condition. I feel very insecure, very vulnerable."

"I can understand that, Eno, it takes some effort to be around people again - you know what? I will pull myself together and get us something delicious from Amukaram's."

The Swami set off for Amukaram's...excited and impatient I waited for the food. I was a little disappointed when he came back only with a half portion of curry rice, two chapatis and two small bananas.

"A bit sparse, Swami, for two men who haven't had a bite to eat in ten days, don't you think so?"

"Don't worry, Eno, I bet you don't even can eat all this. I'm sure you'll have enough by the time you're halfway through."

The food tasted fabulous. Never before have I experienced a meal so tasty, so rich in content, so aromatic - it was a delight for every single taste bud! The Swami was right, after half a meal I was almost saturated. I saved the banana for later. My stomach had probably shrunk a little, the digestion had to slowly settle down again.

After the meal the Swami handed me my passport, my plane ticket and my money.

"Thank you, Swami, it was a very difficult moment when I handed over my valuables to you, because suddenly I didn't know anymore who you are."

"It, was not easy for me either to put you in a state of fear - but it had to be! Only by letting go of everything earthly it was possible to go so far. The letting go of language, food, possessions, the seclusion and the shamanic drink, all this together made this long journey possible."

I suddenly became very tired, laid down on my mat and shortly afterwards I fell into a long, deep sleep.

In the middle of the night I woke up shivering. My head ached, my forehead felt hot. I spent the rest of the night in a twilight half-sleep. In the morning I felt miserable and sick.

"After so much brainstorming a quite normal reaction", the Swami comforted me, "Your calculator is a bit overheated at the moment... it will be fine!"

In the afternoon Caterina visited us.

"Hello Akhenaten, she greeted me warmly and jokingly, "you look as if you have been surfing through all the incarnations at the speed of light."

"Good day, Nefertiti", I replied faintly, "indeed, so it is. I didn't know we've known each other for so long! At the moment I am still a bit worn out and exhausted from the long journey."

"I can totally understand that, Eno, I felt the same way! You know what, I'll give you some Ayurvedic herbal pills - six of them with water every day. You'll be fit again in three days."

The following two days I spent mostly lying on my mat, drinking large amounts of lime water, eating a few *Idlis, Dosas* or fruits, the Swami brought from the village.

I was digesting and processing what I had experienced, reviewing the whole journey once again. I also thought and pondered a lot about my future, my vocation and my love for Erica.

I felt that my time here with the Swami under the tree was slowly coming to an end. The whole story needed time and distance...Would I ever be able to understand what was happening here, what I had experienced here?

Caterina's herbal pills, the care of the Swami and the peace and quiet under our tree did their work. On the third day I was more or less regenerated, and on the track again.

"Hey, Swami, dude, I feel a lot better today, the storm in my head has passed. I've been mulling very much the last two days. I think the time is slowly coming when I have to think about moving on, about saying goodbye - maybe in two or three weeks."

"I feel the same way, Eno, I have the same thoughts. You're young, you have to move on, I'm old, I don't have to move on no more. I am at the end of my journey, this place here under this tree is my last place on this planet."

The following night I dreamt one of those clear, concise dreams that remain dewy in your memory, in your mind, in the morning after waking up...

I was on a gold claim in the Yukon. With shovel and pick I dug a hole in the earth. All around me many other people were digging and slaving. Everyone was desperately digging his hole. Some of the diggers had already dug deep pits, others had hardly started. The digging was very exhausting, the sandy ground crumbled again and again. Resigned and frustrated, I was about to give up when I suddenly came across a piece of leather. The part turned out to be a book in a leather cover. I was happy to have something to read once again...But when I opened the book, there were only empty white pages in it. I was disappointed, and the other gold diggers all laughed at me. As a result, I woke up...happy that the whole thing was just a dream, that I was not actually on a gold claim in the Yukon...

Strange dream, I wonder what it could mean. Why were the pages of the book blank, not lettered, why were they empty? Why didn't they contain a story?

A while of thinking brought the answer...it was obviously up to me to label this book, to breathe life into the empty pages. I alone knew the content, knew what the empty pages contained...They contained the story about my time with the Swami. Writing this story was my vocation! Happy about this realization, I soon fell asleep again.

"Hello, Swami, good morning" I greeted him euphorically, "you know what? I have found my destiny."

"Good morning, Eno, I'm glad to hear that. How and where did you find it? How did it come to you?"

"I dug it up last night, with a pick and shovel. I found it in the form of a book with blank pages. It is my calling to label these empty pages - to breathe life into them! The book should contain the story that we two of us experienced together here under this tree. What do you think of that, Swami?"

"A great idea", he said enthusiastically, "a beautiful vocation! You interpreted the dream correctly! I see you're getting close. So, what about love, Eno? Did you get an answer?"

"I think, Swami, my love belongs to Erica!"

"It's a good sign that you've made progress in this matter as well. - You are under Shiva's favor! He seems to like you very much! Shiva is the god of destruction and renewal. Without destruction there is no renewal - old thought patterns, habits and dogmas need to be destroyed. It is not possible to rebuild on them - that is the principle of Shiva, the original and first shaman!"

The following day, around noon, I took the bus into town. After the long period of fasting, the eternal *Idlis* and *Dosas*, I longed for a culinary change and some distraction.

The Swami could not be persuaded, he preferred to stay under the tree.

"Could you please bring me something sweet, coconut cookies or something?", he asked me.

"No problem, You, old sweet tooth, maybe I can find a Black Forest cake somewhere", I joked.

The Swami swallowed empty, his gaze wandered longingly into the faraway.

"Hey, dude, are you still here? Or would you rather have Strawberry tart with cream?"

The Swami did a languishing sigh. I couldn't help but laughing.

"What are you laughing at, You, malicious joying chap!" he scolded. "Get out of here - and don't come back without sweets!"

Sitting under a parasol in the restaurant Aristo, I enjoyed a mutton curry with a rice side dish and a bottle of Kingfisher beer. Afterwards I took an extensive walk through Pondicherri's French colonial old town, marveled at the magnificent architecture of the buildings and villas. The streets were almost deserted, I felt as if I was taken back two hundred years.

To rest for a moment, I sat down on a bench at the church square. The church bells were just ringing. From a Hindu temple that stood in the immediate vicinity, a drumming could be heard. I was highly taken aback. I was even more astonished that the beat of the drum matched the swing of the bell. Suddenly, from a nearby mosque, the muezzin started singing. Wow...with open mouth and big eyes I was sitting on the bench, I had never heard anything like that before! The muezzin fitted perfectly into the bell and drum beat. There was no dissonance. It sounded beautiful and harmonious. I was really moved - that was real ecumenism! I wished the whole world was sitting on my bench right now. Every polarizing politician and religious fanatic should hear this now - preferably on LSD or magic mushrooms. These people would be in a psychiatric hospital afterwards or forever purified!

Because I was not allowed to face the Swami without sweets, I bought two pieces of nut cakes for us.

"Hello, Eno, old dude", he greeted me when I was back, "you're just in time for vespers, just got some fresh coffee, I hope you brought some sweet stuff with you?!"

"Sure, I did, you old sweet tooth, without sweets I wouldn't have dared to come back at all!"

The Swami poured the coffee into the cups, I unpacked the cake. Smacking and sipping we sat together. The Swami was beaming over both ears, praising the cake in highest tones.

"My Grandmother, Eno", he said with full cheeks, "came from Dresden. At Christmas she baked *Christmas stollen* and gingerbread - man, when I think about it...seventy years ago now!"

In the evening we played another game of chess. This time I tried a particularly clever tactic, but as always, the Swami was even smarter.

The following day began wonderfully, it was one of those days where harmony, beauty and peace merge together, where one is in harmony with the Creator and the world. Already before sunrise we sat meditating in the lotus position in front of our tree. On the horizon you could see the first pink glimmer. For a moment the world stood still, holding its breath...then, the first golden ray. Slowly, majestically, proudly and powerfully the sun rose from the dark sea. The following Yoga exercises I experienced with every tendon, every muscle, the body connected with the mind through the breath.

We enjoyed the following breakfast at Amukaram's. On the way back we bought two big drinking coconuts. Afterwards we went swimming and bodysurfing in the sea again.

Knowing that my days with the Swami under the tree by the ocean were numbered, I now enjoyed everything double and triple.

"Oh, Swami, I think I'll stay here, never go back. I don't know what I'm gonna do in Switzerland. My heart is aching. I can't even think about it."

"I understand you well, Eno, but I think you have to take care of Erica and your vocation now!"

In the evening we sat together by candlelight, chatted a little, let the day end. Then we wished each other a good night and rolled ourselves into the blankets. Peacefully I fell asleep to the distant sound of the waves.

"Hey, Eno...!" The Swami suddenly called, waking me up from a dream. "I think the cobra has bitten me."

I opened my eyes and saw the Swami sitting in the light of a candle.

"Uhh...Swami, oh man, don't joke with me, midst in the night!"

"No joke, Eno, come and see this."

By the candlelight he showed me his left hand, which was slightly swollen.

"Look here, on the back of the hand, those two punctures here."

Indeed! One inch below the ring finger, on the back of the hand, two small punctures were clearly visible.

"How could this happen, Swami?"

"I woke up, I had to go to pee, it was pitch dark, it's a new moon, I lost orientation and instead of heading for the exit, I walked in the wrong direction, right into the damn brushwood pile, then I stumbled and fell right onto the pile. It must have happened while I wanted to get up again, I felt the bite clearly, but I thought it was cacti or thorny bushes. It didn't hurt much I peed then and I laid down again. The hand started to hurt more and more and became more and more numb, then I lit a candle to have a look."

"How long has it been since the bite, Swami?"

"I guess maybe more or less half an hour."

"What, so long?!...the poison is already in your bloodstreams Swami, - you need a doctor, a serum, quickly! I carry you backpack up to the road, we stop the next car – emergency case! I give the driver a good baksheesh, he drives us straight to the hospital."

"Eno, don't panic, just don't start stressing. The poison, as you say, is already in all the bloodstreams. Maybe I'm lucky, maybe it didn't bite down hard - either I survive it or I don't. At this hour you can wait a long time on the road, the drive to the hospital takes half an hour. You know Indian conditions. It may take a while before a doctor comes in the middle of the night with the appropriate serum - forget it, I'm staying here! I don't feel like dying in a moving car or on the tiles of a hospital, I'd rather die here, peacefully under our tree. Over here I can space away in peace on the visions of the cobra venom."

"Swami, you can't seriously want that, let's at least try it - think of Lisa, she will be back soon!"

"Eno, I will stay under this tree. The Great Spirit will make the right decision - I am an old man, my days would be numbered anyway."

"Swami, you're eighty-two, and damn well together, you'll be easy ninety-two!"

"Eno, you're a tough nut to crack! I'm dying and not you, and I want to die the way I want to!"

What could I do? The Swami could not be moved - I could not force him! I understood his logic very well. Still, I had trouble just doing nothing, just waiting around.

For a while I said nothing more, lit another candle and the petroleum lamp.

Suddenly a cramping twitch ran through Swami's body, whereupon he laid down.

"Swami how do you feel?"

"I'm cold, like a fever - from the bite site a burning, creeps up my arm, in my right leg I have no feeling anymore."

"Oh, shit, Swami - man, what should I do?"

"Just stay calm, Eno, don't get upset."

"I really want your coolness, Swami...!"

Again, it twitched spasmodic through his body.

"Oh, dear, the poison is getting in. Eno, I think that was a high dose!"

I took Swami's hand in mine. Quietly, with his eyes closed, he lay there.

"Eno, this is my last journey", he said softly. "The Great Spirit has just told me. He has taken the form of a silver male and a golden female cobra. The golden cobra told and explained me everything. The silver cobra always answered my questions. In the end, the two united. And I realized that they symbolize the intertwined double helix of the DNA. The collective consciousness of the entire universe is recorded in the DNA. Yoga and shaman techniques are tools to communicate with our DNA."

The Swami straightened up, sat cross-legged. From his pouch he took out the brown-bound, gold-marked *Bhagavad-Gita*. I lit three incense sticks, sat down opposite the Swami, somehow, I felt very solemnly, even also in a very melancholic, sad way.

Between the pages of the Gita, the Swami took out two one-dollar bills, which he handed over to me.

"One is for you, the other for Erica," he said, "I was going to give them to you when you leave, as a farewell gift, but now it looks like I'm leaving before you.

These one-dollar bills are personal tickets to a magical event, a special party that you and Erica are invited to. If you look closely, you will find your name on these tickets and Erica's name as well."

I held the dollar bills in my hands, on the front, George Washington looked at me deeply in the eyes. At the back, from the top of the pyramid, the Sirius eye winked at me confidentially. NOVUS ORDO SECLORUM, it was mysteriously written. Underneath it was written in huge letters ONE.

I frowned my brow, I didn't know exactly how to interpret Swami's statement, in any case I couldn't recognize my or Erica's name anywhere.

"Read ONE backwards once, helped the Swami along..."

ENO, I read in amazement.

"Now look at the other ticket", he said laughing, "you'll find your girlfriend's name there."

I turned and reversed the dollar bill, read all the words back and forth - nowhere could I make out Erica's name.

"Hold your index finger on the AM at AMERICA" he helped again.

"ERICA, hey, Swami, I can't believe I missed it. Swami this is very mysterious, say, what does all this mean?"

"All I can tell you, Eno, it's gonna be a high-carat top party! The Great Spirit will inform you in time when and where the event will take place."

Exhausted, the Swami laid down again. He gasped and rang for breath...It almost tore my heart out, to see him lying there like that - fucking cobra! I was about to burn down the fucking brushwood pile.

The Swami was now noticeably worse, beads of sweat covered his forehead. His hand was very swollen, the bite mark had turned purple. I realized that the cobra had caught him full. The hundred pounds Swami had no chance against this dose of poison - that was too much!

For some time, I sat cross-legged next to him, holding his hand. Every now and then I dabbed the beads of sweat from his glowing forehead with a damp cloth.

"Eno", he then said silently, "Tell Amukaram when I have died. He'll report it to the undertaker. There's enough money in my bag to pay for the cremation."

I swallowed...

"You are like my son, Eno, I love you very much. It was an honor to know you. I would be honored if you would preside over the fire ceremony. Give Lisa and Caterina my best regards, tell them I love them with all my heart."

The Swami squeezed my hand a little tighter...

"Eno, goodbye...take care of yourself... see you on our home planet..."

"Goodbye, Swami, old man, I love you. I thank you endlessly for all you have given me and wish you a good journey with all my heart!"

The Swami closed his eyes forever.

I don't know how long I sat next to him, immovable, frozen to a stone pillar...

When the deep orange sun emerged from the sea, my tension dissolved. The pain and grief overwhelmed me... I cried unrestrainedly.

A new day dawned in India - without the Swami!

When I was reasonably calm, I went to Amukaram, who was about to open his food stall. Amukaram reacted very dismayed and broke out in loud lamentations when I told him of the passing of our friend.

In no time the sad news spread throughout the village. The people, a few moments ago still busy and chatting, now looked sad and concerned. No one could really grasp the message yet.

Amukaram offered me a coffee, which I drank silently in small sips, I was unable to eat anything.

He told me that the cremation would take place that same evening, he would organize everything necessary, take care of everything, I should not worry, I should best go back to the tree and wait.

Amukaram's wife Usha, handed me a folded big white cloth... I knew what I had to do with it...

I went back to our tree. The Swami laid peacefully on his raffia mat as if he was sleeping. For one sequence I hoped the whole story was just a dream that you didn't have to believe, that you could shake off.

"Hey, Swami, dude, wake up - time for breakfast!"

Unfortunately, the dream could not be shaken off, did not disappear, did not dissolve.

With a heavy heart I spread the white cloth on the ground. Gently I picked up the Swami, he was as light as a feather, laid him smoothly on top of it. Once again, I looked into his face, put his palms together for an Indian greeting. Then I wrapped the ends of the cloth over him. For a long time, I sat beside him, apathetic, absent, unable to move

I hardly noticed when Caterina sat down beside us. Silently we held hands... I was glad not to be alone anymore. At some point I told her what happened last night.

In the late afternoon, the cremator came by, dragged a lot of wood with his bicycle several times. I helped him unload it and pile it up.

At the sight of the dead Swami, he who had to deal with death every day, he broke out into loud wailing, punched himself on the chest with his fist. When he had calmed down, we lifted the cremation site together, covered the hollow with a layer of wood and straw. Carefully we bedded the dead Swami on it, carefully covering him with the remaining wood.

Caterina prepared the clay slab, which she spread on the pyre in a thick layer as a heat shield. In the meantime, about a hundred men had appeared at our cremation site. They all paid their last respects to the Swami. I was overwhelmed, struggling with tears all the time.

Bernhard, the anthroposophist, was also present. He handed me the photos he had taken of the Swami and me a few weeks ago. (One of them is on the cover of this book).

The cremator now said a long plaintive prayer, which he recited in a monotonous chant. Thereupon he handed me a clay jug with kerosene.

I got wobbly knees - just don't weaken now...I circled the pyre three times, sprinkling the kerosene from the clay jug on the wood. Then the cremator handed me a burning torch with which I lit the pyre. With the burning torch in my hand, I stood in front of it - began to sing the holy *Om*. Slowly the mourners joined in, found themselves in a collectively tone - the ancient tone of the holy *Om*. I was deeply moved, deeply touched, deeply affected. The condolence of these people meant infinitely much to me. Nobody took offence at the fact that I, like the Swami in the end, was a white man from the West, a non-Hindu - only the Indians are capable of this tolerance, this generosity and acceptance!

When the last sound of OM had faded away, the mourners departed. Only the cremator, Caterina and I were left by the fire. After we had eaten something, the cremator also said goodbye. For a long time, we looked each other in the eyes, hugged each other firmly, wished each other all the best for the future.

Caterina and I sat by the fire all night long, smoking ganja *shilums*, holding vigils.

That night Caterina and I made love for the first and only time. It was a beautiful, gentle, deep, melancholy union. That night we gave ourselves the most precious gift of two loving people... the full expression of the soul... There was not much talk. Too much, each one of us was occupied with his own grief, his own thoughts...In the early hours of the morning, just after sunrise, Caterina also said goodbye. It was a heartfelt, moving farewell. We exchanged addresses, promised to stay in touch. Caterina took Swami's bag and a few things to give them later to Lisa. I kept the chess game and the roll of rice paper with the 24 rules of the game as a memory.

Now I was all alone under our tree - a part of me wanted to stay here forever!

After one hour, I pulled myself together, looked for some pieces of bone in the still hot ashes, wrapped them in a silk cloth and buried them together with the trident under our tree.

Then I packed my bundle and said goodbye to my Shaman Swami and the Tree of Knowledge. For the final time the footpath from our tree, passing the draw well, where I had met Shanty from time to time, to Amukaram's food stable, was the hardest walk of my life!

After I had a coffee at Amukaram's I also said goodbye to him and his wife Usha. This farewell was also very difficult, all three of us cried.

With a rickshaw I drove to Pondicherry, checked into the Amala-Lodge and let a travel agency confirm my return flight. Then I went to the post office, where I posted a telegram with the following content:

DEAR ERICA - PLEASE WAIT FOR ME - I AM - COMING HOME ON 23.4. - I LOVE YOU – ENO